**Also by Leandro Herrero:**

The Leader with Seven Faces
Viral Change
New Leaders Wanted: Now Hiring!
Disruptive Ideas
Homo Imitans

# HOWEVER

## WORK COULD BE REMARKABLE

### LEANDRO HERRERO

MEETINGMINDS
IDEAS WORTH PUBLISHING

First published in 2015 by:
**meetingminds**
PO Box 1192, HP9 1YQ, United Kingdom
**www.meetingminds.com**

ISBN Paperback edition:
10 – Digit: 1-905776-15-2
13 – Digit: 978-1-905776-15-3


A CIP catalogue record for this title is available from the British Library.

To Aisling and Thomas

# TABLE OF CONTENTS

## PROLOGUE            I

However people and Therefore people
I make my best clients restless. I make the others comfortable.

## GETTING THINGS DONE            7

## CRITICAL THINKING            43

## LEADER'S CORNER                                      87

# SPACE 137

# IT'S PERSONAL 157

# STRATEGY 177

# CUSTOMER 207

# ORGANIZING OURSELVES 225

# MOBILIZING                                                       271

# CHANGE     319

# CULTURE     351

# EPILOGUE

In praise of borders. The border diet: A Fitness Plan for the Self and the Soul

# DO SOMETHING WITH THIS BOOK

 THINK

 SHARE

 NOTE

 PRESENT

 APPLY

 SUBSCRIBE

 TAKE ON TRIP

 BOOKMARK

 REFLECT

 DISCUSS

 HAVE A CUP

 FOR OTHERS

# PROLOGUE

# HOWEVER PEOPLE AND THEREFORE PEOPLE

Many years ago, I got into Decision Analysis at the hands of my good friend, Dr. Larry Philips of the London School of Economics. I learned not only the techniques, but also the whole conceptual and philosophical framework behind decision analysis.

One thing, above all, got stuck in my brain: the relentless need to seek, bring and assess options. Suddenly I learned that the world before me was richer than it appeared, especially in the rather matter-of-fact business environment. It may not sound like a big deal, but options were under-stated in the scientific environment within the pharmaceutical industry in which I was working at that time. "*How come?*" you may ask. Bear with me.

If I had to write a 'Theory of Everything' on 'Views of the World' through the lens of a chapter on 'Decision Making' and I had very limited space, this is what I would say.

There are two types of people: 'Therefore People' and 'However People'. The 'Therefore People' think this way:

*"We've got data on A, the results on B, the views of C, what we have learned before from D and resources E. Therefore we must do X."*

'However People' think this way: *"We've got data on A, the results on B, the views of C, what we have learned before from D and resources E. Therefore it looks like we should do X."* – At this point, usually 3:45pm, there is great hope in the room that the meeting will finish just in time to catch the 6pm plane back home. – *"However, we could consider Y and Z as well, because although all the variables are solid, we have not taken into account other criteria. Ladies and gentlemen, we have options, we don't have to just do X!"*

Needless to say 'Therefore People' and 'However People' tend to drive each other mad. [By the way, always beware of the 3:45pm syndrome. It is usually at that final part of the day, when somebody launches a grenade such as *"I think the question we have been trying to answer since 9am in the morning is the wrong question"*, or even *"But what is the strategy? We don't seem to have one!"*]

In my experience, for every 'However' person I find three or more 'Therefore' ones. Some scientific and technological environments are 'Therefore Cultures' (believe me, it sounds counterintuitive). Some corporate environments fuel the 'Therefore' further with the collective obsession with 'closure', with 'getting a resolution', 'making a decision', 'reducing uncertainty at all cost'. In the Therefore Benign Dictatorship, 'However' people are very irritating and a bit like second-class citizens.

I wish I could claim here that there is a 'Therefore' and a 'However' gene that would explain the differences between people. I am cynically sympathetic to the idea. But I know that there are hundreds of social factors that shape the way our brain heuristics work and that it starts as early as our primary education.

My favourite word for my work with organizations is 'possibilities'.

Possibilities need 'However' thinking: the need to look at options, to expect some contrarian views, to re-frame questions and do anything else that would prevent you from falling into the trap of the single-track of one view, one path.

Perhaps we could just accept that, in many circumstances, there is only a clear 'therefore' in waiting. That would be sensible. However…

## I make my best clients restless. I make the others comfortable.

My work as an organizational architect entails exploring avenues; it is not simply dumping a dictionary of templates with my clients. With my team, we bring organizational design, leadership and change and management innovation expertise. But we don't have off-the-shelf answers. We certainly don't have complete 'houses' ready, in search of a spec to match them.

I am more of a jungle guide, an explorer and certainly more of a cartographer. The 'organizational houses we build' don't have standard plans. Of course, windows are windows and bedrooms are bedrooms. Translated into organizational terms, there are fixed things. We don't reinvent the wheel. Unless in those instances where the wheel is not a wheel. It looks like one, but it's another kind of round thing.

The best clients want and love the building journey. Every bit is a discovery. Growth is fast and exciting. Risks? Yes there are some. But we fully live the development of the organization, of its leadership and behaviours, of its processes and systems. I bring ways to accelerate that journey. We are all a bit exhausted at the end, but, my God, was it worth it! And when you look back, you can see that mutual trust rocketed.

The other clients want answers, possibly quick. They want to shorten the road to the destination and they want to know what exactly that destination looks like. And if possible, they'd like to get there on Wednesday the 22nd. That does not make them bad clients, just not the best.

These clients want comfort and want to pay for comfort. The best clients want the best, comfortable or not, and they suspect from the start that the journey may be a bit stressful. This does not make them masochists. They simply don't want to settle for the unexamined comfort.

There is a parallel with leadership. If your leadership makes you very comfortable, you may need to have some extra reflection. It's not that comfort is sinful. It's simply suspicious. As for me, when the best client is restless, that makes me feel comfortable that I am doing my job. When the other clients feel very comfortable... now that makes me restless.

# GETTING THINGS DONE

## INTERNAL EMBASSIES

## DECLARATION OF INTERDEPENDENCY

## EFFICIENT INEFFICIENCY

## SMALL THINGS

# GETTING THINGS DONE: 'RELATIONSHIPS' VS. 'STRUCTURES'

A while ago, a telecom client complained to me about his particular division, which seemed to work entirely based on 'relationships'. People got things done because of their own strong networks and highly cultivated personal connections. That was the ethos and the style of the place. His complaint was: "*We need to have more structure and rely less on people's relationships. This is too fluid, too personal. We are a proper company, for goodness sake!*"

Around that same time, another client said the opposite to me: "*We are a well oiled machine where everybody knows what to do, when and with whom. It works! But, hey, I wish sometimes people tapped into their own internal networks more, made things a bit more human. We are people, not systems!*"

In both cases things seemed to 'work'. What is clear is that each of these organizations were (and are) very different, particularly in the kind of people that their workforce is composed of.

9

Hire a 'structured person' for an environment where people cut across barriers, sometimes bypassing processes, to use their personal relationships and you will see this person won't last very long (or that his mental health will suffer after a while). In contrast, to navigate in a 'relationship-driven' culture, you need particular leadership skills, not just technical or professional ones. Rely only on the hiring of 'skilled people who have done it before' and they will not necessarily understand the expectation of 'liaising in person' with perhaps a large network!

I told those that complained of 'too much reliance on personal relationships' that many people and organizations would love to have this in place. But I do recognize that, although the 'relationship-driven' environment may be a very enjoyable and successful one, it can also be tiring for even the most astute of relationship builders, who, at some peak moment of stress, might wish that 'a well-oiled machine' took care of things, on its own...

The title of this piece contains the word 'versus', which implies an opposition. Many of you may think that this should not be the case, that 'we need both'. This is a legitimate position even if it's a bit of 'default thinking' (we all tend to want everything). But the reality is that both environments don't marry well.

Most of the problems we have in organizations come from expecting something from somewhere (people, processes, structures, leadership) that can never be delivered. It pays to pay attention to the 'culture in place' (whether a culture was shaped intentionally or evolved organically and then grew 'on its own'), to have a realistic picture of the type of business execution that can be expected.

There is more than one culture that 'works'. The question is 'how' it works. Then, the next question is, which culture do you want? That is, which kind of 'how'? And leaders should care about the 'how' as much if not more than about the 'what'.

"IF YOU PUT THE FEDERAL GOVERNMENT IN CHARGE OF THE SAHARA DESERT, IN 5 YEARS THERE'D BE A SHORTAGE OF SAND."

These were Milton Friedman's (1912-2006) unkind words about governments. The leader of the Chicago School of Economics, Nobel Prize winner in Economics and father of monetarism, had little time for them.

His point is an important one when applied generically, as I'm doing here with organizations. Any function, or any firm, can manage resources well, but could also screw up completely and even deplete them. So many times the thought has come to me when observing some companies: "*These guys are making money despite themselves.*"

We have all witnessed companies going out of business despite being pioneers in a sector. They had all the sand they wanted. Many things can go wrong, of course, but killing Kodak, for example, belongs to a higher category of bad leadership.

The Public Sector has a reputation for 'sand depletion' - as Friedman suggested - which, in my experience, is unfair, although some examples are notable. The Private Sector on the other hand has the reputation of 'sand conservation' (and enhancement of the shareholder value for the owners of the sand), which is similarly unjustified. Just take a look at a list of companies and market fiascos ('sand depletions') and you'll see most are in the Private Sector.

The truth is that good and bad management, and leadership, runs across most sectors and geographies. With all respect to Mr. Friedman, when you put some guys, Public or Private sector, in charge of the Sahara Desert, anything can happen.

One of the problems we have is that Public and Private sectors don't learn from each other as much as they should. Depleting sand is not the exclusive patrimony of either. There are good and bad sand leaders on both sides and there are big deserts and small deserts. Some people build, some destroy. Some people sustain, some deplete.

# THE TYRANNY OF THE SMALL THINGS

Grandiose plans get sabotaged by small things.

Many years ago, I was involved in what was going to be a thorough and expensive overhaul of the entire IT system of a Research and Development division of a top global pharmaceutical company. The new system would entail seamless cross-collaboration, trans-continental real-time work and simultaneous, multi-country access to a library of information bigger than the entire Library of Alexandria, if there was one today. The usual users groups and focus groups were in place to extract 'the customer's needs'. And so we did.

The number one customer request was: *"Could you fix our laptops? They are so slow\."*

Recently, in a Viral Change™ programme that I was leading in the US, we did an extensive cultural assessment with our usual focus groups, extracting behaviours and other cultural elements. The aim was culture. Ambitions were high. The number one insight that my team received was: *"The new owners (my client) have taken away the free coffee\!"* And this was driving the low credibility for anything else we were trying to do. They seemed to be saying: "*You want to talk about trust? I want to talk to you about my free coffee!*"

Ignoring/neglecting the 'small things' is very dangerous. Many 'small things' have traditionally been left out at the expense of the 'big things', because the thinking is that surely, this is not a priority. But it is.

Call it tyranny if you will, but often the 'small things' are in control.

# [04]

# A BIT OF INEFFICIENCY CAN BE VERY EFFICIENT

Cost-cutting, cutting to the bone, cutting resources down to the bare minimum is praised as efficient. But it's not. Once all the resources have been reduced to a minimum, a series of unintended consequences are seen. People who used to interface with 5 others, now have to do so with 15. The personal touch or intervention becomes mechanical. A sense of exploitation decreases employee engagement. Corporate memory disappears. Knowledge transfer is impossible. And I can list more than 20 other negative consequences.

The problem is that because it has been crafted under the banner of 'efficiency', it becomes politically incorrect to challenge it.

Overlapping jobs, shadow roles, some slack and even some reasonable duplication may in reality be very efficient. It provides the cushion needed for knowledge transfer, organizational learning, contingencies, rapid reaction to customers and, above all, a fluid human fabric that can be employed in a flexible way.

The 'centralization' of services 'at any cost', the avoidance of duplications (even small ones), the resourcing without slack of any kind, is a fundamentalist view of the organization that only people who have never run an organization (and you can find lots of them in Big Consulting Groups) will recommend. It's a non-sense mantra that only pleases people who mistakenly see the company for a spreadsheet.

The cost of the cost savings is a very poor ROI. An extremely efficient company without slack would not get my money.

# ALL-INCLUSIVE? GO WHERE THE ENERGY IS

Many times in my consulting work, I find myself facing this dilemma. Do I involve many people on the client's side, engage them, teach them about 'behavioural change principles' or 'behavioural DNA', for example, and create a journey of many travellers to reach some conclusions or destinations? Or, do I go semi-solo, reaching the same shores, with the same happy CEO and the same professional fees?

Journey 1 can be painful. And it often feels like 'herding cats'. The organizational and behavioural side of consulting has this peculiar problem: everybody thinks they know. People with little or no psychological background become behavioural experts overnight. Managers who have never managed to create any serious traction in the organization, suddenly say that they have been doing this - whatever 'this' means - for many years.

I've never seen non-financial managers claiming huge accounting expertise, or non-engineers claiming manufacturing or mechanical systems proficiency, but I have encountered numerous people in organizations claiming complete understanding of human behaviour, individual and social. Everybody seems to have some sort of unofficial PhD in Organizational Behaviour.

Journey 2 - full provision of hands-on expertise, advice, active involvement, without pretense of democratic participation or over-inclusiveness - is far easier and less stressful.

Some time ago, I shared this dilemma with a good friend and client, an excellent CEO, and he said: *"Do what I do. Go where the energy is and forget the rest."*

There are choices. Bringing people along on a journey can hardly be dismissed as trivial. But one has to accept that it's not always possible to have everybody 'aligned', to use a bit of managerial jargon. Inclusiveness is a noble aim, but it can turn into the pathology of over-inclusiveness very easily.

Some people have an extra need to embrace everybody, or as many as possible, all the time. They are not content with the few, or even with a pure 'rational understanding' of the issues. They need fully emotional, all-on-board, and, if possible, happy, personally engaged people. And they don't get tired of it in the process. Bill Clinton was this kind of man when he was president. For all his shortcomings, this was his fantastic strength. He did not want you to just 'agree' to X, but he wanted you to emotionally love X.

I have to say, I have not seen many leaders like Clinton in organizations.

Inclusiveness should not be an automatic goal, especially at the expense of bold progress. It deserves good critical thinking of what is possible and realistic. In the meantime, I recommend going where the energy is.

# FULL OF EMBASSIES:
## THE COMPANY IS NOT AN
# INTERNAL DIPLOMATIC SERVICE

People in organizations spend a lot of time representing somebody or something else. It sometimes feels like the company does not have employees, but ambassadors.

Project team members represent their functions at the team level. Project leaders represent the team at Portfolio Management meetings. Functional heads (Engineering, Sales, Marketing, Strategy, Communications, HR…) represent their functions at Management Teams. Business support functions (Finance, IT…) represent their tribes everywhere.

Issue 1: some arrows point in the wrong direction. The VP of R&D, member of the Leadership Team, thinks that he represents R&D at the (company) Leadership Team. That's why he switches off (e.g. looks at his Blackberry) when there is no R&D topic being discussed. However, the VP of R&D should in fact represent the company (and its Leadership Team) at the R&D function level (division, staff). If he wanted to be an Ambassador, he has chosen to represent the wrong people. Note: this is not a semantic trick. Representing my tribe at the company level is not the same as being the ambassador for the company with my tribe.

Issue 2: Every company has tribes (sub-cultures). Being part of the tribe has its advantages. However, the ultimate goal of engagement is that the employee represents himself or herself. You have been hired as Maria Smith, but as soon as you get the label of 'Safety Supervisor', you will cease to be Maria Smith so that you can look like a proper Safety Supervisor. Again: not a semantic trick. 'Being oneself' (authenticity) is not the same as 'representing oneself' (my own human capital).

In our Viral Change™ programmes, as soon as the champions/activists have been identified (according to a set of strict criteria) and are called to help, they cease to represent anything (geographies, functions, cultures, affiliates) other than themselves. Occasionally, and symbolically, we give them a business card with their names, but no titles. Very frequently we hear: "*It's about time that the company is asking me to help out on something because of who I am and how I am, not based on my job description.*" Believe me, a bunch of Activists representing themselves and united by a common good, works like dynamite. A bunch of Ambassadors representing somebody (a function, geography, their bosses) collectively has zero power. There is a choice.

Of course, we all represent others, in one way or another. But if your job is representing, not doing, acting, thinking, engaging or using your own human capital, then you are in the Internal Diplomatic Service, but without the perks.

The journey from a company of ambassadors to a company of agents and activists is a great journey. But you may have to close some internal Embassies.

# [07]

# WHY EMAIL IS A CLASS A DRUG FOR THE MIND

The addictive properties of email (as we normally use it) can be explained by the laws of behaviours. Shall we take a short tour?

There are several types of behavioural reinforcement. Regardless of the technical terms used in Psychology, here are some that I have re-named:

Type 1: 'The carrot always ready'. A behaviour is reinforced every time it appears. For 'reinforcement' read 'reward' (monetary, non-monetary), although it is technically not the same. For example, the person does something good, the person gets 'Congratulations, well done'.

Type 2: 'The Salary'. The reward (money in this case) comes at a fixed time (or interval, in technical terms). Your salary arrives on the 30th of each month, no matter what. Lousy job, great job: salary still comes in.

Type 3: 'The Slot Machine'. The reinforcement or reward comes to you in a random and unexpected way. You are doing a good job, but you may or may not get a 'thank you' or a reward. From time to time, though, it comes. You can't predict it. You just know that it will come at some point. It's a slot machine system.

There are more types and variations, but let's consider these three. Type 1 ('carrot always ready') loses power very quickly. By the third time that your boss says 'Congratulations, well done', you are beginning to suspect that you report to a parrot. When this is happening every Wednesday at 4pm, you can be assured that your boss does not have a supernatural memory, but a pre-programmed system of saying congrats (or an excellent secretary). Type 2 ('the salary') is nice, and though it does not come every day, it's good because it's predictable. You don't have to worry about it. As a behavioural reinforcement it's pretty bad though, because it rewards both good and bad performance. Type 3 (the 'slot machine') gets you hooked, because you may or may not get something, so you keep trying. The prospect of getting it, keeps you going. When you get something, you feel your prospects will increase, so you keep trying.

Any (good) student of Experimental Psychology will tell you that Type 3 (the 'slot machine') is the most powerful of all behavioural reinforcement types. Read that as: 'greatest addiction potential', well above any other type. Well, the way we use email is perfect for this. When email is 'always on' and emails are pushed to your Smartphone or your computer screens, announced by a blip, you go to that screen to see if there it is something important. Most of the time it isn't, but at every blip you go back, just in case. Because occasionally you do get that message from your boss that you must not miss, a piece of relevant news, something you need to react to, something 'important'. So, you continue to look at the Blackberry or Smartphone (blip or no blip) just in case there is something you need to do. If those important pieces would always come at 3.45pm every day, you would not be looking at your Blackberry constantly. It is the randomness of the reinforcement (the randomness of the slot machine) that makes you addicted to email.

If you are in a permanent state of checking your email on the Smartphone or Blackberry, you are actually addicted because, statistically, it is impossible that you will find a relevant piece of information every time you check. The more randomly these arrive, the more addicted you will be.

Everything said here about email applies to most social media. You can extrapolate the argument easily.

Cure? There is only one. Limit the inflow to pre-determined windows of time. That is, check only at more or less fixed times. Never keep it 'always on' or 'pushing'. If you could do this and infect your entire team with this behaviour, and if they could do the same with others, your collective mental health will flourish and you'll probably get more work done.

I am not talking here about 'email etiquette'. There are hundreds of guidelines about that. But a very simple frame to understand what works and what doesn't in behavioural terms. Unfortunately, the email addiction is hard to conquer, because it uses the strongest reinforcement type.

And whilst we are on the topic, why don't you un-couple bonus and fixed time, (e.g. Christmas bonus), make it random. You now know why.

# ALL TEAMS WITH A SELL-BY DATE

Imagine that any new team comes with a 'sell-by date'. A label that says this team will disband, no matter what, on the 12 of December. The team has an initial formation date, but also an extinction date.

One of the problems many organizations have is that they create structures, such as teams, with the hope of providing a platform for collaboration, but these structures are open-ended. There is no sense of when the team will cease to be. Rationally, you would think that this is when objectives have been achieved. However, these objectives may be long-term and vague, full of more concrete, short- term milestones. Teams tend to drag on in existence. We put time limits on external contracts, but rarely on internal ones.

You'll have many reasons to see this as non-sense. If the team is at its peak performance, do I mean it disbands anyway? Yes, I do! If there is still obvious work to be done, does it disband? Yes, it does! You'll say this is crazy! But why?

You can make any provisions you want for a second team to take over (yes, you can share previous membership, perhaps even just part of it), but you must declare the team finished and celebrate. Then you can start a new team with another 'sell-by date' the following day.

Perhaps this is an opportunity for a change in leadership, a review of lessons learned, a membership swap, a knowledge transfer that needs to take place (because the crew changes) versus languid knowledge, only reliable in its documented form. Perhaps you can have some new crew members shadowing old team members for a few days or weeks.

After counting the reasons why 'this will never work', imagine the benefits of a constantly renewing team structure. If your main concern is 'disruption' and 'instability', I agree with you. This is precisely what it creates, by design.

But look at the other side: complacency is gone, knowledge transfer opportunities are high, professional development is broad and people's minds are fixed on delivery.

Our organizations have become 'teamocracies' with a life of their own. The team is a vehicle, not an end onto itself. Sell-by dates will restore some sense of focus.

Our Disruptive Ideas' Accelerator masters this and 29 other ideas to challenge status quo and inject innovative thinking...

"THEIR **RELATIONSHIP** CONSISTED IN DISCUSSING IF IT **EXISTED**"

This is a two-line poem entitled *Jamesian* by Thom Gunn (1929 – 2004).

That's it.

I don't need to remind you how many meetings, how many discussions, how many analyses of pros and cons, how much brainstorming are like the 'discussing the existence of the relationship'. But, do we have a strategy? Do we know our mission? Are we a team? All legitimate questions. As are the adolescent questions: Are we friends? More than friends? Or what are we?

Intellectual recycling is extensively practiced across many organizations every day. Antoine Lavoisier (1743-1794) discovered the Law of Conservation of Mass. It says that matter can change form, mixtures can be made, but the total amount of mass remains the same. A more popular version says that matter is neither created, nor destroyed, only converted.

Being in the mode of *"Their relationship consisted in discussing if it existed'* ensures that recycling of ideas and of issues is permanent. It's our Management Law of Conservation of Irrelevant Topics.

Incidentally, something that Lavoisier, the father or modern chemistry, did not manage to conserve was his head. He was guillotined in Paris at the age of 50 during the French Revolution.

# [10]

# THE USEFULNESS OF THE USELESS

Nuccio Ordine, an Italian professor, has written an essay of this title, to my knowledge not translated into English. It talks about the usefulness of knowledge, which has no immediate translation into specific, practical benefits. Perhaps the kinds of things that make us better human beings, but don't have a strict, immediate material payoff. Ordine is talking about the Humanities, or philosophy, or those disciplines that are disconnected from the obvious 'monetary return'. He talks about the concept of 'useful' being only understood as something that has to do with a profession, with an application and, above all, an application with monetary outcome. Ordine says that *"the modern man, who no longer has time to dwell on useless things, is bound to become a soulless machine."*

If there is a sector of society where this concept of utility is taken to this extreme, it is perhaps business and the business organization. The traditional 'effective' organization, conceived as a machine, is obsessed with effectiveness. Therefore, anything that has no obvious 'utility' is bound to generate antibodies. Here is a list: informal conversations, duplications of or shared roles, debates, free-floating time, etc. Even

29

'brainstorming, blue- sky thinking' conceived as a free space for ideas, requires us to justify it with an immediate summary and prioritization. Fear of leaving things without 'closure' is high and even considered a sign of 'bad management'.

We are supposed to be effective, concrete, practical, sharp, simple, outcomes-driven, conclusive and decisive. There is no room for the 'use-less' time where there is no obvious practical outcome. It is, at the very least, simply politically incorrect to behave in that way.

However, the constrained, machinery-like approach to organizational life is missing the point. It kills creativity and innovation. Detractors of the 'use-less', 'no obvious outcome' say that the risk is inefficiency and waste. They tend to see the issue in black and white, where only a certain type of black is good management.

But the presence of some 'use-less' space and time may be key for the ultimate usefulness. Leaders should protect 'use-less' spaces as much as they can, because they are as vital as oxygen to any organism.

# THE LAST THING I NEED IS CREATIVITY

Henry Ford is quoted to have said, *"Why is it every time I ask for a pair of hands, they come with a brain attached?"* The modern version of this is, *"I don't need creativity, it's the last thing I need. I just need people doing the stuff."*

Sure! There are repetitive and mechanistic jobs that need to be done in a repetitive and mechanistic way. You don't want people reinventing the wheel. However, for those jobs, you should seriously consider a robot. It's much better: no health insurance, no holidays, no team building and perfect employee engagement scores.

In the kind of economy we have and will continue to move towards, it's going to be impossible to distinguish between the brains and the hands. They are increasingly going to come attached to each other all the time. The old dichotomy 'Strategy' and 'Execution' will more and more become only a semantic one. Brains and hands won't be separate. The distinction between the thinkers and the doers will be gone. So, be careful what you wish for, you might get more than what you were expecting.

# [12]

# GENE AND TONY ARE COMING NEXT WEEK

If you work in a corporation with headquarters and affiliates scattered in many places, or even with international sites, you will be used to the ritual of 'visitors' coming from those headquarters on a regular basis. Indeed, you, yourself may be, or have been, one of those visitors. Those visits may happen in the context of a business review, or the annual business plan, or simply happen on a more or less regular 'visit schedule'.

Some clients, speaking from the receiving end, don't call this 'visiting', but 'descending' from headquarters. Some half-jokingly (but only half) pointed out to me, that they were considering setting up a proper Visitor Centre given the amount of disruption, hassle and complexity associated with dealing with these 'visitors'.

Some, of course, love to have visitors. It tends to end with a good evening meal, who knows maybe even some good wine and possibly other extras. Others hate it, because it forces many people to focus on 'the visit' instead of on 'the business'. Preparing presentations for Gene and Tony is often seen as an ephemeral and pointless piece of work, but …'it's important to keep them happy'.

You need to see these visits and the whole hoopla around them as a ritual. And rituals stick because they are rituals. They serve a purpose, though usually not the one that is declared and apparent.

Think about what could be behind the visit ritual. It usually covers the whole spectrum: from genuine interest and help, to a waste of time and corporate tourism. But, above all, think about four or five non-declared reasons for those visits. Read between the lines. Try to imagine what other purposes these visits may serve. Do Gene and Tony need to be comforted (that things are going well)? Do they come to exercise a bit of power? Do they think you need more help than you think you need? What purpose does the visit serve for them?

You will find more than four or five reasons. You need to list them and consider them on their own merits. Then, use the ritual and participate in it with deeper understanding. In any case, my advice is not to fight it. When rituals go, other rituals take over. Perhaps you can, gently or not, use the time to explore the value of those 'presentations'. Perhaps you could put yourself in the shoes of Gene and Tony and imagine how 'the visit' allows them to exercise control. Then, ask yourself, why do they feel the need to 'control'? Just because they are 'managers'?

What would you do differently if you were Gene or Tony? At some point, maybe a budget cut is necessary – another ritual in its own right – and Gene and Tony are not coming anymore. See what is going to substitute for this ritual. Something will. Of course the obvious is the conference or video call. Observe and learn how the new 'visit' has changed meaning. Or how it has not. The point is to reflect, ask yourself what is behind or underneath things all the time. Never take these visits at face value. You'll miss a lot of meaning.

[13]

# IS THE CREATIVE WORKING UNIT **THE PAIR?** IT WOULD BE WORTH EXPERIMENTING WITH

# GETTING THINGS DONE

Joshua Wolf Shenk's book entitled *Powers of Two* (2014) makes an interesting case for what the author calls the end of the isolated, single 'genius'. He sustains that behind the single name there is always a second name. He quotes Paul McCartney and John Lennon together with a string of other duos such as Monet and Renoir, Freud and a mostly unknown Wilhelm Fliess or Martin Luther King and Ralph Abernathy. I think that not all the examples are equally strong, but there is a compelling case for exploring the potential of the 'power of the duo', that which Wolf Shenk calls 'the elemental collective', 'the root of social experience and creative work'.

The pair, however, does not need to be invented or discovered. It's always been there. The police cops we see in American films and TV series come in pairs ('partners', sometimes playing 'good cop, bad cop'), as they do in other parts of the world. In my home country, Spain, the police duo was called 'la pareja' and that was also the language used to refer to police in general. If you called the police, you would always expect 'la pareja' to come. Examples could be extended to many other examples of human activity, including priests, nuns and missionaries.

In organizations, the uptake of 'the duo concept' has been a lot slower, largely because of the obsession with efficiency and the terror of duplication. Two people assigned to the same job is considered a waste in traditional managerial terms, period. So any attempt to look into potential benefits is blocked from the start. However, in some parts of the world, some hospitals have been experimenting with the 'pair of nurses' looking after the same individual for a long time. More recently, the work done at Menlo Innovations, in Ann Arbor, MI, has been portrayed in a book by its CEO Richard Sheridan, entitled *Joy Inc* (2014). The software company uses the pair as the unit of work.

It seems that when explored and used, once the barrier of the 'inefficiency' claim has been overcome, the benefits are significant. Knowledge-sharing, productivity, perhaps speed,

**35**

social learning, etc. they all come back positive again and again.

'The pair' would deserve a good double-blind study in your organization. Translation: choose an area or division of some size, install the pair as a unit and see how it goes compared with others. And there is another reason why I would do this: it's the very concept of experimentation. That's something we do very infrequently in organizations where default positions are very strong and unconventional thinking is often unwelcome.

The pair is a good organizational hypothesis in search of brave experimenters with an open mind.

# TO SAVE EVERYTHING, CLICK HERE (AND ITS VERSION INSIDE THE COMPANY)

'Clicktivism' is the term used to describe the type of pseudo-activism that consists of clicking the 'Like' button (mainly on Facebook) and feeling that you have completed your contribution. It is usually an unkind, pejorative term (compared to activism) that describes how easy it is to 'click' and forget about doing anything concrete to provide real support. It's a known fact that many societal cause websites, which are often also fund-raising, can get 'Likes' in the hundreds of thousands, but often manage to raise very little money. Clicking is fast and easy, donating is another matter.

*To save everything, click here* is the title of a book by Evgeny Morozov, a fierce critic of the 'internet-centrism' and author of other books such as *The Net Delusion*. The book is a brilliant, polemical, passionate and critical account of the 'dangers' of the above-mentioned clicktivism.

With my organizational architect's hat on, I can see parallels within the organization, even though we don't have the

37

equivalent of the 'Like' button for engagement, ideas, projects, etc. Perhaps just as well! But we do have equivalents of clicktivism in the occasional internal epidemic of over-inclusiveness: 'I agree' and 'Fine with me' are email 'contributions' that we could do without. 'Fine with me' is particularly pervasive. It often means: that's my contribution, done. I don't really have to do anything else. It's the Facebook 'Like' button in the company's information flow.

I don't need to say that there are many instances when this is legitimate. We all have used this before. But I always suspect 'internal clicktivism' when I see reams of my clients' emails with lots of well-intentioned people replying 'Fine with me' (or the equivalent) to a colossal distribution list.

To agree with everything, send the email. 'Yes-tivism'?

# INDEPENDENCE IS DEAD. WRITE YOUR DECLARATION OF INTER-DEPENDENCE

There was a time when writing a Declaration of Independence was the climax of an identity quest. This is a theme I have written about in the paper version of my TEDx talk in London and which you can read about in the epilogue of this book.

In organizational terms, nothing that we do is independent. We are hugely inter-dependent. I ask my clients, whether they are at CEO level or head up a division or management team, to write down their Declaration of Inter-dependence. Mastering inter-dependence today is mastering the firm; it's another word for management. Business today has no other choice: Independence is dead.

Inter-dependence allows you to define your space (social, managerial, commercial, purpose). It is by understanding inter-dependence, not independence, that one can create one's own identity. What you are, the space you occupy, what distinguishes you, is no longer something you can do in isolation, pretending to be independent. Independence works in exclusion mode. Inter-dependence works in inclusion mode. Inclusion is not agreement. It means making the most of the shared views of the world and also being very clear about the differences, the different views of the world. It's not one or the other; it's both what unites us <u>and</u> what separates us.

It's tempting to extrapolate this argument to the 'independentist' movements of the day such as the Scottish and the Catalan ones, though both are very different. Any nationalist and 'independentist' position (and both things are different) have a 'thought trap' built inside: equating independence with identity. So what is sold to the masses is the package: if you want to preserve your identity, you have to be independent. It's one of multiple populist bundles that ensure a particular answer to any question about either identity or independence. 'Independentism' may indeed, be a legitimate position with a long list of arguments, but 'identity' is a false one. An identity that needs independence as an exclusive factor for survival is a weak identity.

On the business side, inter-dependence is the only way. Complete independence creates silos. Silos hate collaboration. Without cross-collaboration there is no firm today. Identity (the firm, the division, the internal group) without interfaces, tensions, commonalities, differences, customers, colleagues, inter-dependence, agreed non-negotiable behaviours, etc. is nothing more than a logo, a colour code, a letterhead.

# CRITICAL THINKING

OR LACK OF IT
SWITCH OFF THE
AUTOMATIC PILOT
MIND TRAPS
**THE WHY AND THE
'HOW TO'**
LANGUAGE

# MANAGEMENT 'POST-HOC FALLACIES': DAMN GOOD STORIES!

The Latin 'Post hoc ergo propter hoc' is freely translated as: B follows A, so A must be the cause of B.

It's a fallacy. We installed that piece of software and since then, the computer is very slow. Therefore, that software is causing this performance issue in my PC. We have just come back from a trip abroad; one of the kids now has a serious fever and is sick; she must have got food poisoning from that last dodgy restaurant.

Since everyday life is full of 'post-hoc fallacies', there is little point in giving more examples. There are plenty of them. And not surprisingly, 'post hoc fallacies' also dominate business life.

All people in the sales force have gone through the new, expensive sales training programme that lasted six months. Our sales figures have markedly improved. That sales training did the trick.

Joe has taken over as the new CEO, after the rather disastrous year with Peter at the helm. The stock price has rocketed. Joe is the right leader, the market always knows.

We have gone through a one-year, intensive Employee Engagement programme, with multiple initiatives at all levels, and what happened? The overall company performance this year has been brilliant and the overall employee turnover halved! Another example of how Employee Engagement pays off.

These are three real stories from my consulting work with organizations. And 'stories' is the right term. Damn good ones too, I have to say. But without exercising some critical thinking, these stories may remain at the stage of fallacy.

The sales training may have been excellent, but the markedly improved sales figures could also be explained by a pathetic performance of the main competitor, who completely screwed up their greatly anticipated new product launch.

Joe may, indeed, be what that company needs as a CEO. But the stock price success could also be explained by a cost-cutting programme that Peter, the disastrous CEO, had started before he left and which is only now starting to show results. No offense, Joe.

The Employee Engagement is a great initiative, but instead of leading to brilliant company performance, it could be that the brilliant company performance (based upon a series of successful launches) shaped employee satisfaction and sense of pride. This may be why people scored so high in many parameters in the Satisfaction Questionnaire. A halo effect.

A fallacy is only a fallacy until one looks critically at it and explores alternative thinking. Left unexplored, they may be very good stories of success, but the arguments behind them may or may not be true. When, in my speaking engagements, I challenge audiences to think of potential fallacies in our arguments, I am conscious of the fact that I am daringly pushing sensitive buttons. No Training Manager wants to hear that their programmes may or may not have had the attributed impact. The same goes for Investor Relationships, or the Board of Directors, or HR.

Taken to the extreme – people tell me – we would not do anything, since (according to me, they say) we can't prove much in Management. But this is a narrow view of why we should do things in management. Sales Training programmes need to take place, perhaps CEOs need a replacement and there is nothing wrong at all with that Employee Engagement programme. We do all these things because we believe in good management and because we are paid to exercise judgement. Don't stop doing them!

Exercising critical thinking and practicing good management are not in mutually exclusive! Not all good stories of success contain a fallacy. But spotting management fallacies can only lead to a better management. The key is not to settle for a good story.

# WHO WOULD YOU TRUST WITH THE WEATHER FORECAST? THE INDIANS OR THE WEATHER SERVICE?

It was autumn and the Indians on the reservation asked their new chief if it was going to be a cold winter. Raised in the ways of the modern world, the chief had never been taught the old secrets and had no way of knowing whether the winter would be cold or mild. To be on the safe side, he advised the tribe to collect wood and be prepared for a cold winter. A few days later, as a practical afterthought, he called the National Weather Service and asked whether they were forecasting a cold winter. The meteorologist replied that, indeed, he thought the winter would be quite cold. The chief advised the tribe to stock even more wood.

A couple of weeks later, the chief checked in again with the Weather Service. *"Does it still look like a cold winter?"* asked the chief.

*"It sure does,"* replied the meteorologist. *"It looks like a very cold winter."* The chief advised the tribe to gather up every scrap of wood they could find.

A couple of weeks later, the chief called the Weather Service again and asked how the winter was looking at that point. The meteorologist said, *"We're now forecasting that it will be one of the coldest winters on record!"*

*"Really?"* said the chief. *"How can you be so sure?"*

The meteorologist replied, *"The Indians are collecting wood like crazy!"*

This 'Old Indian tale' is neither old nor Indian. Circular thinking is part of any organization. I am sure you'll find stories of 'cause and effect' in many areas of the business. Many actions, strategies and plans are based on 'most people are doing X'.

Well, let's remember the Indians!

# [18]

# I CAN PROVE ANYTHING IN MANAGEMENT THINKING

I can't remember where I saw this. And that's partially my point. It could have been anywhere. But I am sure it was in a prestigious business journal, one of the few must-reads for fear of missing that important business wisdom assertion that could change the route of your business forever. I am sure the statement is correct because I noted it down:

*"Companies that outperform have strong values, a strong sense of purpose and excellent execution."*

There you are. Strong, unequivocal findings from the 'Global Study of the Most Whatever Companies'.

I found it on an old, small, yellow notepad, which tells me it must have been written down in a US airport on one of my recent travels. I also wrote something below it, something I personally added to the 'findings' (probably to improve them!):

*"They also have toilets, car parks and a coffee shop!"*

It must have been my irritation with the so-called 'research', which is something that has flooded management thinking. Anything can be proven, especially anything that suits your need for logic.

Ephemeral findings like this, dominate management. Strong values, sense of purpose and excellent execution? Sure, I'll take it. Outperform the ones with weaker values, no sense of purpose and bad execution? Sure! And your point is?

I am sure there is a case study coming up. After all business case studies are a bad form of journalism. Oh, and also, people in the outperforming companies mostly have two legs.

# [19]

# LET'S ELEVATE THE CONFUSION TO A HIGHER LEVEL

There are times when you get stuck in arguments. Discussions seem to go nowhere. You are going around in circles and it's not obvious what to do. People around you - in a meeting, for example - don't want to abandon the discussion for very good reasons. Despite the fact that it's not going anywhere, the subject is not trivial and you want to come to some sort of resolution.

There are many things one can do, but here are three that will cost you nothing:

One: take a serious break
Two: tackle a completely different topic and come back to this one later
Three: reframe.

Number three is the one I'd like to talk about here.

It has to do with using new lenses and changing your mental frame of mind. The best way to start this is to use the most powerful Weapon of Mass Disruption we have in management. That is to ask the question: *"What is the question (that we are trying to answer)?"* If you are lucky, that alone may get you un-stuck, because a great deal of the running-in- circles-and-going-nowhere may simply come from the lack of clarity about the question on the table.

If, however, the problem still persists, change the question. Play 'What if the question was different?' What if the question was not the one we have formulated, but an alternative one? Some examples: We are stuck on the question of profit. What if the question was how to gain market share? We are stuck on the question of employee benefits. What if the question was employee engagement and retention? We are stuck with using a leadership model in a performance management system. What if the question was not about assessment, but about the way we develop these leaders?

Surrounding the original question with alternative questions, all of them close enough to the original (but not the same question simply rephrased), may suddenly do the trick and provide a road map to answer all of them.

These three real examples, which I have recently dealt with in my work with clients, may seem like trivial changes in the questioning but they are not. The little reframing involved has great power to disrupt the thinking and provoke fresh ideas.

The main problem with being stuck is being stuck. Moving in any reasonable direction is much better than running around in circles. The alternative questions and the 'what if' will take you out of the vicious circle. Sometimes I call it 'elevating the confusion to a higher level'. Or a lower one!

Change the frame. It does a pretty good job.

[20]

# PRESERVING THE PROBLEM WHEN DEDICATED TO FINDING THE SOLUTION.

It's called the Shirky principle, named after Clay Shirky, the prolific American author of bestsellers such as *Here comes everybody* (2008) and *Cognitive Surplus* (2010). He writes and consults on the impact of the internet and other social topics. The principle reads: "*Institutions will try to preserve the problem to which they are the solution.*"

Commentators on the Shirky principle, which was articulated in 2010, often associate it with other 'paradoxical' principles. The one I really like is Upton Sinclair's (1878-1968): "*It is difficult to get a man to understand something when his salary depends upon his not understanding it.*"

Some organizational cultures are solution-focused. They pride themselves in solving problems. So, they have lots of them. They need them, obviously. Dedication to problems (to solving them) could result in admiring them. In admiring them, problems may be prolonged, perhaps perpetuated. So they can be solved. This is how systems work. In a funny way, you could say.

It's easy to create a structure around problem solving and the structure then becomes the problem itself. On simple reflection you will find hundreds of examples of this. Just to refer to one of those, the matrix organization was created as a way to solve the problem of Divisional and Functional groups or units not talking to each other. When the matrix became a mantra, a form of organization that 'everybody should have', it also became the real problem based on its own complexity. But it perpetuated itself because it was 'the solution' to an older problem.

Structures, processes, systems and 'functions' in organizations tend to preserve their own existence. This is not even conscious or malicious. It's an automatic mechanism in a system such as a medium or large enterprise. The issue is not to criticize this, but to acknowledge that this is 'always' happening.

Bureaucracy, group-think, recycling of data, over-inclusiveness are all potential symptoms of 'problem preservation'. They are in front of us all the time. We don't need a doctor to tell us that we have the symptoms. But the Upton Sinclair principle may apply: we may blind ourselves to protect our own interests.

Only self-reflection, critical thinking, the ability to realize that maybe the problem is now us can lead to the health of the system.

We need to question whether the structure that we have created to address a problem or a challenge is becoming a bigger problem than the one we are supposed to solve. Perhaps, sometimes, a problem un-solved is better than a whole structure trying to solve it.

# THE GREAT 'HOW TO' TAKEOVER

There is a period in child development when children start asking the question 'why?' They usually seem unsatisfied with only one answer and keep asking, *"But why?"* Education is supposed to take those 'why?'-questions and amplify them, use that early explosion of curiosity in the mind, make sure that it is welcomed and nurtured, and guarantee that this curiosity stays forever, beyond the initial big bang.

Bad education, however, misses this opportunity completely and instead of pushing for a permanent 'why?', rushes to offer a great quantity of readymade answers that seem to progressively decrease the need for more 'why?' The mind says: *"There seem to be answers everywhere, particularly from that long, rectangular space on the screen called Google search, so perhaps I should not worry so much."* Neil Postman (1931-2003), a US educator, put it as sharply and as unkindly as: *"Children enter school as a question mark and leave as a full stop!"*

There is a point in the child's education when the 'why?' loses the battle and the 'how to' becomes king: this is how you answer the question, this is how you do it, this is how you solve the problem. At some tragic point, the 'I know how to answer this' in the child's homework, becomes totally independent of the question.

I call the point of inflection, when the 'why?' enters into prolonged agony, even exile, and the 'how to' takes over, the big 'How To' takeover.

Education, from the Latin 'educere', means to extract from within, to take out, to come to light, to set the 'why?' free. I call the opposite of this de-education: to give all the answers beforehand and promote the 'how-to' over the 'why?' De-education teaches how to produce beautiful answers, regardless of whether they are the right answers to the questions.

Given our education system, it should not surprise us that there is a whole industry of 'how to' products and services, from publications to consulting and life coaching: how to be happy, how to be successful, how to be a good parent, how to bake a cake, how to deal with rejection and a myriad more.

In that context, it should not surprise us either that in organizational life (a reflection of society, after all), we are working mostly with the 'how to' currency. Skills, competences, entire HR systems of performance management are designed to deal with people who know 'how to' do things.

The 'Why are we doing this?' is in flagrant short supply. The reasons why we do what we do are assumed: there is a strategy, a dictation, goals, a process. The focus is on how to deliver. Some people told me: "*I am paid for doing stuff. Nobody has ever suggested to me that I am paid, or will be paid, for asking why.*"

# CRITICAL THINKING

The problem accumulated is certainly not the richness of the 'how to', but the poverty of the 'why'. Asking 'why are we doing this?', even if it requires the courage to confront dozens of pairs of eyes looking at you in disbelief, is a disruptive idea, a provocative, healthy intervention for which one should get a good bonus.

# [22]

# "NEVER TRY TO TEACH A PIG TO SING. IT WASTES YOUR TIME AND IT ANNOYS THE PIG."

Robert A. Heinlein (1907-1988), American science fiction writer, was famous for his quotes. This is one of them. Many uses and interpretations of it fall on the unkind side. Applied to people, well, you get the picture. But it also brings several other messages to the table:

- Persist in doing something that will never produce fruit.
- Having people (sorry, he said pigs) in the wrong jobs.
- Being resilient for the sake of it, as opposed to 'fail fast' and move on.
- How being stubborn is rarely a good idea.
- The overall futility of pursuing wrong avenues and expecting them to turn out well.
- How in many cases the only outcome is the duo 'waste of time' and 'annoying somebody'.

# CRITICAL THINKING

Reliability is not stubbornness. One of the arts of leadership is being able to switch gears at the right time and being able to say: wrong path, sorry, now this is next. Another part of being a good leader is to make sure people are in the right places (skills, competences). And knowing and finding out which ones are right is another leadership feature.

There is a common practice in many organizations that consists of moving people around to different jobs. It is often noble and can be useful for obvious reasons. But many times in my professional life I have seen the abuse of this when the rotation of people becomes a mantra. Critical thinking should come first. In many cases, this mantra does not teach the pig to sing and the result is that they will both become very annoyed.

Intellectual tourism around jobs may sound great, but it has its limits.

[23]

# NOTHING
## THAT REQUIRES
## PITCHING IN AN
## ELEVATOR,
## IS WORTH
## PITCHING

# CRITICAL THINKING

I am sorry to disagree with the conventional wisdom about the 'elevator pitch' that says that one has to be able to describe a mission in life, a purpose of business, or a portfolio of products in the 20 seconds of an elevator trip. I don't buy it. Not even if the elevator is in the New York Empire State Building. Or even better, in the Burj Khalifa in Dubai, the world's tallest building.

The pressure today is to summarize, condense, shrink, highlight, make as short as possible. There is a quest for cleverness, synthesis, the slogan, the sound bite, the PR line, the brand's power-line, the smart tagline, the 'one sentence', the 'three bullet points', the summary, the executive summary, the key points, the short version. Sorry, I don't buy it. And I know it will make me unpopular and politically incorrect.

There are short and long things, simple and complex, reducible and not, long and short. And, there is a place for both, but the world is saying, there is only one way: the short, the 'elevator pitch'. Of course, we find ourselves in the midst of a full pandemic of Collective Attention Deficit Disorder, but it does not mean that you have to contribute to the illness. Sorry, I am not going to do it.

Clear thinking does not correlate with length of sentence. Ernest Hemingway's writing has been hailed as the norm of modern English because of the very short sentences he used. I believe that he wrote everything in short sentences because he was mostly drunk and could not write a long one. I met him once in Spain for 5 seconds. I was 10 years old and I remember the hotel terrace where my father used to take us on a Sunday afternoon and where Mr. Hemingway was having some fun.

If it's worth pitching, explaining, if it's appealing, convincing, engaging, enchanting, don't use the elevator. Opt for the longer journey of the conceptual stairs.

# [24]

# YOUR MIND MAY TRICK YOU. THE TRUTH WILL SET YOU FREE.

You have bought a pair of very expensive tickets for a classical music concert, but the traffic is horrible and you are late. They won't let you enter into the concert hall until the next break. Never mind, the first piece of the concert wasn't that important.

You've bought a jumper online. It was a bargain. A big well-known brand with a reduced price of 60% off the retail price. The jumper arrives. The quality is not great. You suspect the jumper is not an original. You say to yourself: *"The colour is very nice though, it fits perfectly, it shows the brand, and, quite frankly, for what I've paid, it's great."*

You expected that promotion you thought you deserved. It entailed having a team of people working for you. Promotion time comes, but you are bypassed in favour of somebody else. You think: *"Thank God, because it would have been a nightmare to have to manage people; I could do without that pain."*

You have just hired Peter to lead that division and he is now a full member of your management team. Peter came with the highest credentials; he interviewed very well and represents just the right addition to your senior team. Three months in the job, Peter has managed to generate widespread antibodies. His management style is blunt and unpleasant; you get many expressions of concern and some real complaints from others. The choice has been, quite frankly terrible. But you say that Peter is misunderstood, he brings lots of value and people need to be patient. He is the right man at the right time for the job.

In all four examples, your mind is protecting you so that you can bear the discomfort produced by the gap between your expectations and the reality, your decisions and the outcomes. It's a helping hand to allow you to feel less of a fool, or not a fool at all. It was really bad to be late for that expensive concert, to get a terrible quality jumper in the post, to fail to be promoted and to hire Peter. But your mind comes to your protection with a different version of reality in which you are no longer a looser, but, actually, an incredibly clever winner.

Psychology has a name for this phenomenon: it's called cognitive dissonance. Your mind has this ingenious mechanism for avoiding the unpleasant and instead producing perfect 'assonance'. Lousy decisions are converted into smart ones, mediocre outcomes into 'the best thing we could do in the circumstances', bad mistakes into 'the greatest opportunity for learning'.

Life in the organization is full of this stuff. You can't avoid it. You can't stop your mind behaving in that way. That's why critical thinking is so important. Critical thinking is often in short supply in organizations where the rush to do, and to be seen doing, induces in us the tendency to bypass a great deal of logic. In haste, cognitive dissonance is an even bigger problem: it makes it easier to justify many things that perhaps are not that justifiable. Once the decision is made, there will be plenty of reasons to justify it as a good one. In a hurry, or under stress, this happens in automatic pilot mode.

But there are simple protective measures at hand. For example, bring more options, bring more diverse views, make 'alternatives' mandatory in decision making. But, above all, dare I say, 'pursue the truth'. The Biblical 'the truth will set you free', adopted by many in the academic world, should have a similar place in the life of the organization.

Openness, honesty and candour, start with the old expression and Call a spade a spade.

# "THE LIMITS OF MY LANGUAGE MEAN THE LIMITS OF MY WORLD."

Said Wittgenstein.

Language in business and organizations creates frames, but also limitations. And we have lots of these frames. 'Employee Engagement', 'Talent Management' and 'Change Management' for example are common frames for anybody in business, but for an alien they are far from clear conceptual entities. By using a particular language we infer that everybody will have a common understanding of what is meant, but some of these 'concepts' have many varying interpretations.

'Change management' is perhaps at the top of the abuse charts. Its use in IT simply means 'making the new IT system live'. Its use in project management, in mergers & acquisitions and in cultural change, however, has very different meanings. By calling something 'change management', instead of creating a shared understanding, we are creating a limitation of understanding. This limitation of the language creates limitations in the world of management.

Other bits of management dialect that have set up permanent camp in the organizational landscape have become standard jargon which, because of their progressive lack of meaning, as before, creates limitations in the world of management. Try to have a conversation these days on 'empowerment' and you'll see the insecure smiles of people around you, begging for a definition of some sort. And it's better to do just that and define it, rather than continuing the conversation assuming that everybody 'knows what we are talking about'.

Tribal language – and business language is tribal – can't be suppressed; only substituted.

An injection of clarity and plain language would do us all an enormous favour.

# I DON'T KNOW AND I DON'T THINK YOU KNOW EITHER

'I don't know' is a hard statement to make for leaders who are supposed to know it all. That is why many of them make up stories in order to give an answer. We all know people who always have an answer. Margaret Thatcher was a politician who always had an answer which often seemed to be independent of the question.

'I don't know' is a magic, trust-generating statement. It shows that you are human and are not in the possession of the Total Truth. 'I don't know' on its own may not be enough though. It needs the extras. Here are some:

'I don't know, but I will find out.'
'I don't know, but it's a good question.'
'I don't know, can you help?'

And many other variations.

One that I like is 'I don't know and I don't think you know either'.

If said in a friendly and non-aggressive way, it puts everybody (for example, in a team discussion) on a level playing field. It also tends to generate some helpful smiles. Of course it may mean: *"Don't pretend you know more than I do; let's be honest."* It's a call to take a reality check, to land from a 'pie in the sky' discussion, to define a new baseline: that of people searching for answers in an honest and open way.

Are they any other uses?

I don't know.

# GANDHI'S CONCEPT OF WESTERN CIVILIZATION

When interviewed by a journalist and asked: *"Mr. Gandhi, what do you think of Western civilization?"* Mr. Gandhi answered: *"I think it would be a good idea."*

Here are some parallels for us in companies:

What do you think of our Culture?
What do you think of our Corporate Social Responsibility?
What do you think of our Company Values?
What do you think of our Identity?

These and other questions share something in common. They each have a label. But the label is no guarantee for anything. Values, identity, responsibility and culture are all 'concepts' full of rich language. It's not until you de-construct them that you can see the reality of what is actually behind them. In the absence of doing that, they should remain in the 'it would be a good idea' category. Yes, it would be nice to have one of these, so now let's figure out what exactly we mean by this.

Language is a beautiful thing. It is also deceptive. In our organizations, we need to have the courage to define what we mean by things. That is one (and only one) of the reasons why in my organizational work we focus obsessively on behaviours: concrete, visible, with unequivocal meaning.

I use the 'Gandhi question' often with clients. It always works well. It helps us to come down to earth and look seriously at the reality, good or bad. If the answer is, "*well, it would be a good idea to have one of these*", we may just be on the right path to finding it.

# BOTTOM-LINING EVERYTHING IS SIMPLY SILLY

The following line is taken from one of multiple leadership coaching service offerings that you can find on the web. A rather prestigious brand, I have to say. *'Corporate clients are increasingly demanding tangible, measurable results that not only help the leader being coached, but visibly impact on the corporation's bottom line."*

There you are! Helping the leader personally is not enough. You want to show bottom-line impact. Besides, this is an 'increasing corporate demand'. I hope whoever wrote that line is not paid very much.

This obsession with the measurable market results bothers me. Sometimes I am not sure why it does, perhaps because it is so naïve. Perhaps it is this over-selling: *"don't worry, we will provide good coaching, and by doing so, I can assure you that the bottom line will be impacted'*. People saying this have zero credibility with me.

The bottom line is impacted by the following factors: good work, good leaders, the weather, pathetic competitors, luck, the stars, good strategy, bad strategy plus luck, and providence. These are my top 10. I could add many more.

There may not be good evidence that a sales training programme will deliver a 3% increase in market share. To promise this is stupid. However, the lack of evidence should not stop you supporting that type of training, if you believe it's good for your people. You send your kids to the best possible school at your disposal, but I have never heard of any headmaster promising you that your kid will become an engineer. Yet, you chose that school because you believe it's going to be good for them.

We have mistaken the intrinsic and moral value of things with the measurement of results. No leadership coaching system that needs to stress that 'it will impact the bottom line' is worth having. There is intellectual deficiency at its core!

My very best clients care deeply about the bottom line, and I also care about their bottom line, but they don't ask me to prove the impact of what I do on that bottom line. They know that what we do will create uniqueness which will go a long way towards that bottom line. The more one talks about the bottom line – unless you are in specific strategic and commercial discussions – the more one misses the point. It may be politically correct to do so, and may make people having the conversation feel good, but that's all.

# [29]

# WHEN THE ONLY THING YOU HAVE IS A HAMMER...

... everything looks like a nail.

If you have a predetermined view of the performance of people in the organization, if you see it fit into the form of a Bell curve of normal distribution, you will allocate people to that distribution following predetermined percentages. For example, there must be 10% bottom, 10% exceptional etc. You will mold your reality to fit into that Bell curve. Many organizations and HR systems do that.

If you use the Gallup 'only 12 questions' formula to measure Employee Engagement (and this is how many organizations do this measurement), you will look at Employee Engagement through 'Gallup Q12' -eyes and will tend to ignore everything else. A Gallup score will be your employee engagement reality.

If you have a routine of corporate road shows in the form of 'Town Hall Meetings' and this mechanism is well established, you will fit your communication strategy into the Town Hall road shows, with perhaps little concern for their effectiveness. The number of Town Halls will be the measurement of your communication.

If you have a Customer Relationship Management (CRM) system in place, bought and installed at a huge expense, you may end up equating customer focus to using the CRM. You will use the language of the CRM as the language of customer focus.

If you have as Procurement system in place, perhaps designed to source your engineering support needs, you may end up using it to procure anything including a leadership development or a change programme. Even if these programmes speak a Martian language in the eyes of the engineering procurement people.

If you have a sales performance management system focused on numerical targets, this is what you will aim at and talk about, even if you ask your sales people to care about customer insights (there may not even be a 'customer insight' box in the system).

If somebody has made a decision about restructuring in Business Units, all aspects of the reorganization will be tailored to fit the decision, whether it is feasible, or reasonable to 'Business Unit-size' everything.

If you have a strong language, narrative and ethos of 'problem solving', you will do everything to find solutions. You will become proficient at dealing with problems and you will tend to generate more of them, because you are so good at it.

I certify that all the examples above are real and that I have come across them on my consulting path. If the only thing you have is a hammer, everything will look like a nail. Check your hammers, the ones you have and the ones you contract out. Make a good inventory of them.

# [30]

# SAY IT COMES FROM MCKINSEY

A friend of mine and a great management consultant told me once that when he needs to grab the attention of underwhelmed executives confronted with a new set of ideas or a conceptual model of strategy or execution, he simply tells them it comes from McKinsey. *"But you are cheating!"* I said. *"No,"* he said, *"I can link anything to McKinsey stuff."* So there you have it. A series of bubbles and Venn diagrams in PowerPoint, full of more or less standard content, can be elevated to a biblical level by reference to the Highest Priesthood of management consulting.

I am sympathetic with my friend, although I don't practice his trick. A top client once told me, *"if the Board needs comfort, we'll call McKinsey. If they need culture change, we'll call you!"* Which seems to imply that McKinsey can't provide cultural change and I can't provide comfort. Mmm, I guess I should be honoured with that quote, since my organization is only 0.02941176 % of McKinsey's in terms of bodies.

External consultants are Traders of Ideas, Gangs of Executors, Merchants of Comfort or permutations thereof. Brands are often warehouses of comfort. *"No One Ever Got Fired for Buying IBM"* was an 80s slogan. The Board of Directors' use of Very Big consulting firms is their insurance policy. I am not suggesting they would do a bad job, I'm just stating it's a well-known practice.

We can't blame them for having a powerful brand, but that does not necessarily ensure success. Several times, I have witnessed the calling-in of the Big Consulting Firms for purposes which were clearly outside the expertise of those firms. I have witnessed the disbelief of seasoned executives that are told to 'use them'.

Comfort, knowledge/ideas and execution are different things. A good friend of mine is an excellent general practitioner. He makes people feel at ease and that makes his clinical judgment very credible. He is also a very bright professional. That helps. He has a physician as a partner in his medical Practice. Let's call him Dr. Smith. Dr. Smith is also very bright and apparently he was top of the class in medical school. In a mixture of humble attitude and typical British understatement, my friend used to say: *"If you want to get better go to Dr. Smith; if you want to feel better, come to me."*

The same applies to management consulting.

# [31]

# DADYC : DO ACRONYMS DRIVE YOU CRAZY?

Management culture, particularly of the Anglo-Saxon origin, loves acronyms. This is something all new employees need to learn. When coming from another industry or country, it's even worse. But luckily, the learning is not particularly painful. Acronyms are that part of the tribe's language that one needs to master in order to navigate through rituals. And this happens fast. By day three in the new job, corporate speak is usually incorporated.

Soon one will learn that PTSD is not Post Traumatic Stress Disorder, but Project Team Strategy and Development (usually a meeting or team, not a structure), and PMT is not a physiological state, but a Portfolio Management Team.

You can have a quick and dirty diagnosis of the organization by looking at some of their acronyms. If the top team is a CoDir ('Committee of Directors' in France/Spain) or ExCom (Executive Committee), it is not exactly the same as an LT (Leadership Team), for example. It's more than simply semantics.

Of course it's not only business that uses acronyms. Medicine loves them too. It makes it more inaccessible to the Indians so that the qualified Chiefs can keep an appropriate power and distance.

Acronyms also elevate an entity to a higher level. If it deserves an acronym, it must be very important.

When there is something serious going on in the world, from a natural disaster to a terrorist threat, the UK government calls a meeting of a body called COBRA. The TV newsreader then solemnly proclaims that the Prime Minister (or PM to the initiated, because Prime Minister is too long) has called a meeting of COBRA for tomorrow morning. COBRA sounds very serious. It's the name of a venomous snake. It sounds like an attack system, a big reaction in the making. However, COBRA stands for 'Cabinet Office Briefing Room A', which is a bit of an anti-climax, if you ask me. (In the US – I am told – COBRA stands for the Consolidated Omni-bus Reconciliation Act of 1985).

Back to the organization, I think there is a case for handing out a contract to a new employee with an acronyms glossary attached, as part of the induction programme.

Most of speech is tribal, life in organization is tribal and the acronyms are here to stay. GUTIT! (Get used to it!)

# [32]

# THIS IS A NON-SMOKING FLIGHT

If you are a frequent traveller, as I am for business reasons, you will be familiar with the standard safety announcements at the beginning of each flight. This is perhaps a piece of communication for which attention is most required and yet, it is universally ignored, people invariably hide behind the newspaper.

You will know that, at some point, the attendant, or the recording, will say: "*This is a non-smoking flight. Smoking is prohibited.*" And just in case you are incubating some clever ideas: "*Smoking is prohibited in the lavatories*". Don't even think about it, because: "*Lavatories are fitted with smoke detectors*". And if you are on a US flight, it then gets serious: "*Federal regulations prohibit smoking*" and (very, very serious) "*tampering with the smoke detectors will end in prosecution.*" So, if you don't want to end your business trip or worse, your Orlando vacation, with a Guantanamo Bay experience, you know what to do and not to do.

And I wonder. Smoking on all flights was banned in 1998. Why is it that 17 years later I still get the warnings? So, I'm just curious, if this is a non-smoking flight, are they suggesting I could have chosen a smoking one? Where is it?

Many processes and procedures (and, unfortunately their associated jobs) have become robotic. Customer services: "*is there anything I can help you with?*", once you have bought the entire mobile phone package and are locked in for 24 months. Hotel front desks: "*Did you have a good stay sir?*", after you have just complained about bad heating, bad food and very, very thin walls. Supermarket checkouts: "*Will that be all, Sir?*" once you have paid a fortune for two trolleys full of stuff, etc.

Could somebody in the Robot Resources Department of the Federal Aviation Authority and its cousins at the European Aviation Safety Agency (sorry to pick on you) perhaps review the script written in 1998? Or, is this simply maintained by the Tobacco Lobby? Just kidding!

In every organization there is a 1998 rule that is supposed to stop something, long after the 'something' has already stopped. I know this from my years in the pharmaceutical industry, where projects that had been formally stopped years ago, still had some people working on them years later. Every organization also needs to practice and spread a very disruptive idea: ask the question 'why are we doing this?'

I use this often in Viral Change™ programmes. And you'll understand why...

# [33]

# THE CLOUDS MOVE TO FOLLOW ME. THE TRAFFIC LIGHTS TURN GREEN WHEN I MOVE.

These two statements represent a form of magical thinking of the kind seen in ancient humans (clouds) and today's humans (clouds and traffic lights). Today's humans include you and me and also managers.

In fact, the second example ('the traffic lights go green when I move') is typical of a rare mental disorder called paranoia (not the same as paranoid schizophrenia), in which the patient lives a completely shielded reality within his own logic. If, this reality is not in conflict with others, people with this disorder can go about normal life completely unobserved. A patient of mine, many years ago, was convinced, amongst other things, that he had invented the Italian Vespa, but his patents and drawings, had been stolen. Over the years, he had come to the conclusion that it was in his benefit not to fight for his rights. (I had no problem agreeing with him about the wisdom of not fighting). He had all sorts of other collateral, strong and immovable beliefs, but unlike in other conditions, these beliefs did not clash with anything or anybody. So we concentrated our conversation on his headaches.

This type of thinking ('The clouds move to follow me. The traffic lights turn green when I move') has remarkable similarities to some close-to-magic, uncritical management thinking. This kind of thinking gets rid of the uncomfortable and annoying issue of having to distinguish between cause and correlation. Particularly if we want to attribute a success to ourselves, any correlation, plus a little dose of uncritical thinking, can easily be converted into causality. The so-called 'attribution bias' is a good example: *"If we succeed, it's to our credit. If we fail, it's because they are bad."*

When we put ourselves at the centre of all (good) 'causality', we are very close to 'the clouds move to follow me'. 'Our magnificent leadership is the cause of the turnaround in sales'. Certainly not luck, or our competitors being pathetic, or the recently newly super-motivated sales force, or combinations thereof. Of course not! The clouds move because they follow me.

Magical thinking gets by unnoticed in organizations when we dress up the arguments with lots of (correlation) data. Everybody wants to hear good news and everybody wants to attribute some merit to themselves. What's wrong with that? Nothing. But some things, like the alleged invention of the Vespa, are not worth fighting for.

# LEADER'S CORNER
## COLLECTIVE LEADERSHIP
## CHARISMA
## GLOBAL,
## BACKSTAGE

# HIS GREATEST SUCCESS WAS NOT TO FAIL

Many people, many of them in high managerial positions, succeed by avoiding failure. They become unmemorable by design. A new headteacher was appointed in an important school. The press went back to past pupils and asked what they remembered about him: *"He fell down the stairs once."* A new pharma R&D leader is nicknamed 'The Chronic Survivor', because everybody else from his top team has left or has been fired, but he managed to survive all the storms unscathed. People can't remember any mistake he has ever made. People can't remember anything, period, other than the fact that he survives.

These two vignettes are real and part of my past consulting experience. Many leaders may remain un-noticed and in the unmemorable category. They are squatters in the organization chart. 'What do you want to be remembered for?' is a crucial question we don't ask often enough.

# [35]

# THE DEATH OF THE CHARISMATIC LEADER HAS BEEN GROSSLY EXAGGERATED

Like Mark Twain said, "*The death of the charismatic leader has been grossly exaggerated*". The problem is that 'charisma' has changed its face. Many years ago, charismatic leadership sounded loud. A charismatic leader was supposed to mesmerize, exhibit exuberant passion (the stereotype of the American leader?), be extraordinarily persuasive (could sell ice to Eskimos) and be able to command an almost unconditional following. Of course, I am in caricature mode here. It took a lot of time to realize that many exceptional leaders were not charismatic at all according to this profile.

Perhaps charismatic leadership today has a different profile. His or her inspiration comes from being emotionally and socially brilliant. The new charismatic leader sees and feels the social environment around them; they 'get' the people and the dynamics of the organization. He or she is a master of giving the stage to others, something that I have described as Backstage Leadership™. Above all, the new charismatic leaders have less of a 'push' style (messaging) and are more able to 'pull (attract) behaviours' around them. They would be firm and visible, but also far more humble.

I have a little rule of thumb about trust and charismatic leadership. The old type used to trigger reactions such as: "*He is brilliant, great charisma, but I am not sure I trust him, though.*" The new type often first produces an 'I trust this guy' and then other traits follow. But please, don't look for any science behind my rule.

Perhaps new forms of charisma have been evolving all the time, but the death of charisma itself has been grossly exaggerated.

It reminds me of an old phenomenon when I started medical school. Students used to repeat (and shout): "We don't want magisterial lectures" (which are the ones given by professors in front of hundreds of people for sixty minutes or so, non-stop, in huge amphitheatres, as was the norm.) I always thought that the main reason for disliking these lectures was because we did not have good 'magisters'. Had we had good ones, I personally would not have minded at all.

I wonder whether the charismatic leader's recent fall from grace has to do with the scarcity of them.

Just a thought.

[36]

# CAN ANYBODY DISPEL THE MYSTERY FOR ME PLEASE? WHO ARE 'THEY'?

These are commonly found uses of the expression 'they' within organizations:

They won't approve this.
They don't get it.
They don't listen.
I don't know what they would think of this.
They are bad at execution.
They haven't said anything yet.
They really don't know.

And there are numerous others. The use of 'they' is almost mythical.

I have heard 'They won't approve this' in the context of leadership teams referring to the Board of Directors, even when two members of that leadership team were also members of the Board of Directors.

I have heard 'They are very bad at execution' used by management teams to refer to their troops, even when every single member of that collective 'they' reported into somebody in that management team. So, if 'they' report to you, then the problem is you, not them! So, you, actually, are bad at execution.

I have heard 'they don't really know' in a Board of Directors meeting, referring to both external investors and employees. I have also heard the mythical 'they' in the same Board of Directors meeting, with no obvious reference to anybody, leaving me with to question whether the real 'they' that was referred to was the Holy Trinity or any other supernatural entity. I left the meeting without clarification.

If anybody knows who 'they' are (and has their Social Security Number) please let me know, so that I can incorporate it into my organizational work. I would not like to miss them. 'They' would never forgive me.

# [37]

# LEADERSHIP'S SPLENDID EXPEDITIONS

"*The history of mankind might be described by a cynic as a series of splendid expeditions towards the wrong goal or towards no goal at all, led by men who have all the gifts of leadership except a sense of direction, and every endowment for achieving their ends except a knowledge of ends worth achieving.*"

These words by Sir Richard Livingstone (1880 – 1960) still resonate today. His focus was education, but this paragraph should be kept as one of those perennial quotes and pieces on leadership.

The 'splendid expeditions towards the wrong goal or towards no goal at all', reminds us that not everything that looks like an expedition may be worth it. We may make leadership complex and even well-orchestrated, but this also needs 'a sense of direction'. It seems trivial when simply stated like this. I particularly like 'sense of direction' as opposed to a fixed destination. The second part of the statement talks about 'ends worth achieving'. Again, leadership may look like an expedition towards ends, but the additional qualification 'worth achieving' hits the nail on the head.

I have treasured this quote for many years and still it comes back to mind again and again. I use it with my clients within leadership work, individual or collective, as a piece for reflection, even digestion of all of its parts.

The full quote continues with a second part on education:

> "*We must not forget in our education this element, a sense of direction. We do forget it, if we are content that our schools should merely impart knowledge, develop and discipline the intelligence, train character in the narrow sense. They must also be places where the mind is enriched by the right visions and where the ends of life are learned.*"

Educational systems in the Western world are struggling. The 'place where the mind is enriched' is still a goal that remains to be achieved. Perhaps leadership starts in school. Perhaps this is why true leadership is still not well-entrenched in many people in organizations. However, it's also true to say that many people are genuine in their quest; sometimes intuitive, sometimes guided. In the true sense of Livingstone's view of the world, I regard leadership development as 'education'. In the etymological sense of the word: to get, from inside, that which is already there in the person.

I guess many of us, you and myself included, are on some kind of splendid Leadership expedition. It's worth checking if we've got the right maps.

# 38

# 'IT DEPENDS':
## WHEN ETHICS, LEADERSHIP AND VALUES BECOME
# FLEXIBLE AND ADAPTABLE

*"As a partner in the communities in which we operate, we believe the company has a responsibility to conduct itself according to certain basic principles."*

And to avoid any doubt, these principles and values were very explicit: Respect, Excellence, Communication and Excellence. Contained not in a couple of PowerPoint slides or a few posters, but a 66-page manual.

This company had 20,000 staff, 110 billion US dollars in revenues and was named America's 'Most Innovative Company' by Fortune for six consecutive years. I am talking about Enron, which filed for bankruptcy in 2001.

When reading that particular Ethics Code, a commentator once said it was like finding a copy of the Titanic's manual for Safety at Sea.

There are hundreds of accounts of what did and did not happen and I am no expert on the technicalities that led to the fraud. Malcolm Gladwell's *Open Secrets* in the New Yorker on the 8ᵗʰ January 2007, for example, is a good piece on this that I have read more than once.

But from the myriad of comments from every imaginable management angle, including, of course, Enron's frequently quoted value system (as I am doing here as an illustration of the meaninglessness of 'values on paper'), one aspect has recently caught my attention. I confess I did miss this before. It is explained in a 2011 article by David Burkus and I am sure in many other places that I missed as well.

It refers not to the CEO, Jeffrey Skilling, now in jail until 2017, but to Andrew Fastow, the Chief Finance Officer. Burkus says that *"Fastow undertook an elaborate process of establishing special partnerships to bundle assets and secure loans. The board of Enron, understanding that Fastow's involvement in these partnerships was a violation of its code of ethics, voted to suspend the code of ethics' application to Fastow while these partnerships were active. Fastow's actions and the board's decision were not kept private, as SEC regulations required the identities of these partnership members to be disclosed."*

This is a story within the story: (1) Not only did the value system not seem to count for much; (2) it was suspended so that special partnerships could be formed without conflict; and (3) the Board did it and it was out in the open!

This is surely the most bizarre, public, temporary suspension of a Code of Ethics in order to enable the most senior people to be unethical if needed. It is the 'contingency model' in action. The one that says 'it depends'. The 'it depends' model, which appeals to rationality ('situations are different') is very handy. It allows people to deal with uncomfortable barriers. It has always been with us.

Will we always behave in way X? It depends. In India it is possible to do Y, because this is the way things are done there.

Is behaviour Y always unacceptable? No, it depends. In culture Z this is normal, so who are we to judge?

Is ethical policy A non-negotiable? Well, it depends. Because in country B you could not enforce it.

Will our Corporate Social Responsibility be universal? It depends. Region C is not really ready for it.

The old tension between 'Values-Based Leadership' (values and behaviours that are not negotiable) and 'Contingency ('it depends') Leadership' is an old one. It has not gone away. Reviewing the old war stories about Enron when doing my research on ethics and corporations, has brought back the 'it depends' that I have frequently confronted during my business life and that has always driven me mad.

The Contingency Elephant is still in the room, well-fed and alive. An inventory of your own 'it depends' is a good start. Some things change, some must stay no matter what. Some things depend on other things, others don't. And when they don't, they can never have an 'it depends' attached.

# 39

# A LEADER WITH 2.2 BILLION FOLLOWERS

He didn't say much, at least as far as we know. He didn't leave any writings behind. Compared to today's Life Gurus who have vast CD programmes, video collections and podcasts on subscription, perhaps even their own TV channel, he did not have a serious chance of success. He was in office for only 3 years. And nobody knows exactly what he did before that job, other than that he disappeared for a month and a half in solitude (not on a training course), apparently to prepare himself.

Although he was in the religious business, his first management team was composed of fishermen, not learned PhDs or theologians. He used analogies, parables and stories to share his message and vision. No PowerPoint, no bullet points or 'the 10 strategic imperatives are' slides. He did not make any money. He walked around. He wasn't an 'armchair producer of messages'.

He irritated both his family and the powers of the day. He did not mingle with the jet set of the time and preferred those of lowly status. He did speak up. He had a mission. At the end, he was murdered. Not until 70 years later did people start to write his memoires.

This is an impossible CV for a leader. He would not pass any recruitment screening today. But what he started more than 2,000 years ago still continues today with 2.2 billion followers. Mr Jesus from Nazareth as a leader defeats most conventional assumptions.

As his Christian followers start a Holy Week of remembrance in the next days and regardless of your own religious beliefs, it's worth pausing to reflect how much Leadership can learn from the unconventional, the disruptive, the authentic, the purposeful, the humble and the servant.

2,000 plus years later: still going.

# [40]

# IS RUTHLESSNESS A LEADERSHIP STRENGTH?

In times of crisis, people look up in search of leadership, and when looking up, they expect to see decisiveness, resolution and determination. People, who under normal circumstances have a more benign view of leadership, suddenly turn into advocates of dictatorship. *"These are no times for inclusiveness and consensus. Make a decision, give an answer, lead, be ruthless!"*

Ruthlessness is certainly full of adrenaline and, may I say, testosterone. I have never forgotten this example of ruthlessness from the old, now forgotten Bosnian war and have kept the newspaper clipping with me ever since:

> The journalist and the sniper
>
> What do you see?
> Two people crossing the road.
> Okay, which one do you want me to kill?
> Neither.
> Pity, you could have saved one of them.
> (The trigger clicks twice)

# LEADER'S CORNER

Martin Bell, Bosnia, *The Sunday Times*, 22nd December 1996

And you may ask what this ruthless assassination has to do with the surely more benign and non-murderous ruthlessness that we want from leaders in particular times?

Good question. But the brain does not discriminate that well between the mechanisms of ruthlessness. Of course, we are not shooting employees and nobody drops dead on the corporate carpet. But would it be foolish to ask if we are sometimes shooting psychologically, mentally? I have seen many psychological assassinations in my business life so I am very sympathetic to some employees wearing bulletproof jackets in particularly dangerous situations, for example, around those of the sniper-leader type.

I wrote an article a long time ago with the title *It's the system, not me*. This is the worst type of all 'sniper-leadership': I am a good guy, but 'they' force me to inflict this upon you.

No, any leader is free to choose to pull the trigger and shoot, or not. Ruthlessness is not determination. When in crisis and looking up, be careful what you ask for, because you might just get it.

# IT'S **ABOUT YOU** AND **BETWEEN YOU**, NOT ABOUT US AT THE TOP. IT'S NOT ABOUT THE LEADERSHIP TEAM

In one of the multiple accounts of the 2008 Obama campaign, campaign manager David Plouffe wrote in his book *The Audacity to Win* (2009) about the importance of the grassroots movement. This may seem obvious and indeed common to many campaign and political strategies. What was (and remains today) different in Obama-land is the extraordinary emphasis on the transversal, the tribal, 'people like me' connectivity and collaboration. Put simply, the message was a persistent: "*It's about you, talking to other people like you, not about Barack Obama talking to you.*" Of course, Obama did talk to them and indeed with superb rhetoric. So they were not short of top-down messages. But the campaign itself deliberately de-emphasized that, for the benefit of the 'you and between you'.

The 2012 Democrat campaign outnumbered that of the Republicans by several factors of magnitude in 'local clusters' and their 'local organizers'. The total numbers were less relevant than the clustering and the sense of belonging. It was about 'them': those local communities, local offices, local groups and the communication and connectivity between them. Technology only facilitated that, and boy, did it ever.

We, in organizations, tend to dismiss this tribal ('it's all about you') element, perhaps in favour of 'it's all about the objectives, or the strategy, or the guidelines from the top or even the vision'. Obama and Co also had objectives, strategy, guidelines and vision, but they seemed to say, "*Don't get distracted. Focus on that vision, but it is really, really, really about you: how you discuss it, what it means for you, what you can do, how you can involve others.*"

This resonates with our Viral Change™ programmes where we focus 75% of our time on the grassroots, bottom-up, 'people like you' and 'it's all about you' engine of change, and only 25% on the top-down messaging. Messaging is very important indeed, but it is very easy to kid yourself and fill all airtime with messaging, forgetting everything else. Messaging is the 'push'.

Viral Change™ orchestrates the 'pull'. The bigger the protagonist role of the grassroots movement is, the greater the scale-up of behaviours.

A good learning from the political strategists of Obama-land was that no matter how much top-down communication they could provide (and of course, Mr Obama did!), what really mattered was that transversal, local clustering; the 'it's really about you', grassroots penetration. The Obama campaign was extremely successful because it was not a campaign but a social movement. Viral Change™ orchestrates these social movements within the organization and in the macro-societal world.

Viral Change™ was first published in 2006. Obama did not call us, but maybe now somebody could call the White House!

# FOR LEADERSHIP LOOK AROUND, NOT IN RESEARCH PAPERS

Leadership has traditional sources of learning, reflection, role modeling and a 'body of knowledge'. There are four that dominate and this is my humble classification: the military, corporations, civic and religious models and sports.

So where do organizations borrow from for leadership models?

The military source is mostly about language (as opposed to individuals). The language of war is well-embedded in organizational and business thinking: killing the competition, price wars, winning and losing markets, etc. Occasionally there is reference to true military strategy and leadership, but not too frequently. Civic and religious leadership is also referred to, but here with the accent mainly on individuals. 'I have a dream' and Luther King must be the most admired example. Business organizations love sports analogies, which, in my opinion, are over-rated and oversized.

There is a point here, however. There are multiple sources from which to learn, mirror, copy, study and draw conclusions from about Leadership. Multiple models and examples. It was in this context that some time ago, I was invited to participate in a round table on the topic at a prestigious global business school. The Head of Research presented their five-year research data on the Future of Leadership. It consisted of in-depth interviews with most of the chairmen and CEOs of top FTSE 500 companies and extrapolating from these he claimed that they now knew what the future of leadership would look like. That was it! I was quite taken aback.

I put it to them that they had completely missed the point and that the views of the chairman of Coca Cola, for example (with all due respect to the Chairman of Coca Cola), were hardly relevant to day-to-day leadership in organizations. I pointed out that there is a myriad of small or not so small enterprises that are full of people 'leading' from day to day; navigating through life, with different degrees of resilience and most of them

108

without a golden parachute should they screw up. "*Where was that data?*" I inquired.

I didn't like the way he looked at me and I realized that to them, I had just turned into a Martian. I am sure that 'the research team' enjoyed a handsome travel budget and found the interviews with the prestigious leaders and their research rewarding, but to call this the latest on the leadership of the future was slightly insulting to say the least.

Every day we miss the reality that is there, right in front of our eyes, in favour of the big names and big label position papers and reports. For leadership, it's easy: look around. Don't look up at The Big Names. Or don't just look at them. Try schools, neighbourhoods, community leaders, small companies, medium and big, churches, public servants, good CEOs even if they are not on the front page of the newspapers.

We are rich in examples of good leadership. As rich as we are poor in so-called 'research'.

Sorry, it's not about what the CEOs of the FTSE 500 think. Leadership, good or bad, is all around us, because it's a praxis (practice). If we are serious about research in leadership, we need to come down to earth and do a whole lot better than interviewing the usual suspects.

Update: I keep waiting for an invitation to another of their roundtables, but they still haven't called me.

# [43]

# COULD THE GLOBAL TEENAGER TEACH US ABOUT GLOBAL LEADERSHIP?

Today, there are more similarities between a teenager in Shanghai and a teenager in Rome, or Singapore and Madrid, or London and Paris, than you might expect, given the transcultural differences between China, Italy, Singapore, Spain, UK and France. Traditional thinking about geographical cultures focuses on differences. The reality of the contemporary age-related tribes, such as the Global Teenager, is commonalities. How can we reconcile both?

In the world of organizations, the issue of 'global leaders' comes up all the time. What are they? What are their competences? What does one have to have to be or to become a global leader? There are indeed some answers, not surprisingly mainly from the field of intercultural studies led by consultants or academics. But most of these views are based on fairly retrospective data. Often, the answers feel a bit old and suspiciously predictable. For example, we are told that global leaders must have 'cultural sensitivity', which is the equivalent of saying that an airplane must have wings.

I am caricaturizing this a bit, at the risk of annoying a great group of expert colleagues in this area, but there is something about the set of competences for 'global leadership' that makes me feel slightly uncomfortable. The competences are sometimes a sort of mental 'déjà vu'. I have seen them before. Which ones are specific, if any?

I wonder if instead of looking backwards with analytical tools (as is usual in academic research), we would gain far more by looking forward in time and observing the emergent characteristics of any 'global phenomenon'. I suspect teenagers are a good start. They did not receive training on how to be global. How did that happen?

I also wonder if instead of focusing on developing global leaders, we could focus on developing good leaders. If we drop the 'global', will the sky fall? Will new generations of leaders be global if they are good leaders?

Think about the teenager's capacity to naturally gravitate beyond borders to where there is common interest and get on a level playing field with their friends in a non-self- conscious way without paying much attention to where they are located, They are de facto global. The inhibitions of adults and leaders, the preconceptions and clichés are what stand in the way of 'the global leader', but if they are good leaders, this will stand them in good stead no matter what culture their followers or colleagues/peers are from.

# [44]

# FOR EVERY EMPOWERING LEADER, THERE MUST BE FOLLOWERS WHO WANT TO BE EMPOWERED

In all my years of organizational consulting, while I have found leaders who don't empower their people, I have found many more followers who don't take advantage of the empowerment. The conventional wisdom is that there are long line-ups of people in the organization waiting to be empowered. And that the problem lies in the widespread 'command and control' from leaders: they don't empower their people. We all know instances where this is true, but empowerment is a two-way street.

Two examples:
(1) Project teams with a relatively low level of control over their own destiny, are finally given greater control. As part of this 'upgrade', the Project Leader, who has spent years complaining that 'the project team does not have a budget', is given budgetary control. But the now potentially Almighty Project

Leader rejects the offer! The 'no thanks' arguments (or excuses) range from 'too much responsibility' to 'but we don't have financial training'.

(2) Some people are historically excluded from some corporate committees. These excluded corporate functions complain that they are treated like second-class citizens. Eventually they are invited to those forums and given full membership. But these people now complain that they are too busy to attend so many meetings.

These two examples come from my reality, with real names, real companies and, needless to say, real frustration. Frustration that's all the bigger for me, because I have pushed so hard to obtain that kind of empowerment.

Willing to take responsibility and accountability, to occupy an empowered space, is harder than complaining about the lack of empowerment. Inclusiveness is great for preaching, but being included has a price. For many people, when faced with it, they find it too high. The old English saying, "*Be careful what you wish for, you might get it*", should be posted on a sign at the front door of the Empowerment building.

By the way, many people hate the word empowerment, so my apologies to them! But I hope we all know what we are talking about.

[45]

# THE LEADER WHO SAVED MY COUNTRY AND THEN FORGOT WHO HE WAS

Adolfo Suárez, the first democratically elected President of the Spanish Government, died on the 23rd of March 2014 at the age of 81. He was probably the best politician we have ever had in modern Spain, my home country.

If you ever travel to the Parador Nacional de Gredos (a state-run hotel in my native Salamanca), which is in the middle of nowhere in the mountains, go and see a little room downstairs with a small golden plaque on the wall. That little room was once occupied by a few people - fierce historical enemies from the whole political spectrum: from the ex-Franco system to the clandestine communist party - who were voluntarily locked in there together to draft the Democratic Constitution of the New Spain. It was 1978. I was 28.

I visited this room a few years ago for the first time with my family. Nobody was around and I remember my tears. The democratic transition of my country is the most understated and undersold political phenomenon of modern history. And it is thanks to Adolfo Suàrez, a man from the Franco regime, that we could achieve what we did.

He was chosen by the king, against the odds. A member of the old regime with the most unlikely of briefings: dismantle the regime. So he did. He was charming, intelligent, a good man. He legalized all political parties including the Communist Party, which for many embodied the official devil of recent history. He reinstalled the historical local government in Catalonia before any constitutional reform was even in place (a fact that many Catalans have already forgotten). He navigated through a 48h-long tragic-comic coup d'état. He put together a coalition as a new political party for the transition. The party disbanded after a few years once the transition was complete. He never benefited personally or financially. When he left office, he refused to take any salary or any money from the State. He had an overriding theme in mind. As he put it: "*to elevate to political reality, what is reality in the streets.*"

What most eulogies don't say is that he had also been a man of great personal suffering. Both his wife and his daughter died of breast cancer. Two more daughters are cancer survivors today. After leaving office, he lived off his work as a lawyer, but when he wanted to take his wife to be treated in the US, he had to re-mortgage his house. In recent years, Alzheimer's took over. He could not remember people, or facts, or indeed that he had been the man who saved a country, the first President of the new democratic government of Spain.

Political lessons aside, he was a leader who (1) saw the common good above all things personal, political, ideological or party-related; (2) was resilient like bamboo in the middle of a storm; he was hammered everywhere by everybody, those who saw him as a traitor and those who saw him as a fascist; (3) had a mission and embraced everybody, not a single side of society was left out (the exception being the terrorist organizations).

He was a giant. He had the worst possible pedigree: a man of Franco's old regime. He could not have passed a job interview for democratic leaders. He surprised everybody, because he believed in the common good and he had the guts to do it.

How many times do we pre-judge people with 'wrong pedigrees' in our organizations? *"He is an accountant, he won't be a people's CEO"; "She is an engineer, she'll run a machinery of processes"; "He is from big corporate, he can't run a small entrepreneurial outfit",* etc. How many times have we been proven wrong? Suspending judgment would be a good start!

Not many people outside of Spain would know Adolfo Suàrez. He did not make any money from his public work. He did not go on a speaking circuit, nor mingle with global celebrities. He was a good man, an honest man, a transient leader with sense of purpose, with the wrong CV, who, once his mission was accomplished, even forgot who he was himself.

116

# WHERE THERE IS NO VISION, PEOPLE PERISH. WHEN THERE IS TOO MUCH VISION, PEOPLE PERISH FASTER

"*Where there is no vision, the people perish*", says the Bible, in the Book of Proverbs.

This quote comes in handy when you talk about leadership. But I tend to add: "*Where there is too much vision, people perish faster.*"

Leaders with absolute, clear vision of the future and a perfect plan, scare me. I think they are dangerous. Give me a leader with some uncertainty, but determination to succeed and I feel safe. Unquestioning visionaries need opticians, not followers.

My best client leaders have willpower, resilience and contagious properties in their DNA. They speak the language of possibilities, not of fixed destinations. They also like to be judged by their present deeds, now, not by history. They feel the need to serve and respond to their people, not to a Supreme Being, which, together with 'history', forms a convenient, non-reachable duo, out of reach for the scrutiny of fellow travellers. In short, politicians of the genre 'History will judge me' should be banned permanently from any office.

I know of a leader who had a very strong vision, a great Strategic Plan, absolute clarity of where to go, commanded great authority and trust, mastered people engagement, was determined, focused, driven, results-oriented, and forward looking. Last time I checked, he died in a bunker in Berlin.

# I AM A CAPTAIN.
## WE ARE ON A COLLISION COURSE!

This is a great story of focus, determination, appeal to progressive levels of authority... and some other things. We leaders can learn a lot from it.

The lookout on a battleship spies a light ahead off the starboard bow. The captain tells him to signal the other vessel, *"We advise you to change course twenty degrees immediately!"* The answer comes back, *"We advise you change course twenty degrees immediately!"*

The captain is furious. He signals, *"I am a captain. We are on a collision course. Alter your course twenty degrees now!"*

The answer comes back, *"I am a seaman second class, and I strongly urge you to alter your course twenty degrees."*

Now the captain is beside himself with rage. He signals, *"I am a battleship!"*

The answer comes back, *"I am a lighthouse."*

This excerpt, from the New York Times bestseller *Plato and a Platypus walk into a bar* by the inimitable duo, Tom Cathcart and Dan Klein, is a delightful reminder of the dangers of omnipotence in a leader and of the need to listen.

In fact, the captain was lucky that the lighthouse was manned (by no less than a seaman second class). The collision point is not necessarily manned in many businesses. Sometimes maps are not that good. Who knows, maybe maps do not exist, but we are using an old one anyway, just in case. Or the navigation tools have been produced by old Business Schools when they were doing 'research'.

# WHEN MANAGEMENT IS OVERWEIGHT, LEADERSHIP MAY BE STARVING

I must confess I have never been 100% comfortable with Warren Bennis' traditional distinction between leaders and managers. I always thought it was too stereotyped: Managers do things right, leaders do the right thing. However you read it, leaders seem to win…

But there is definitely a point in distinguishing between management and leadership.

I have my own three distinctions:

Managers make sure that the operational machinery works. Leaders make sure that there is operational machinery that's fit for purpose.

Managers take care of the healthy functioning of processes and systems. Leaders ask why we need these processes and systems.

Managers push stuff. Leaders pull stuff.

An overweight managerial system reigns when most of the airtime is given over to processes, systems and procedures. Note that I am not saying this focus on processes, systems and procedures is wrong. I am saying it could be given too much weight and steal all of the airtime. When this problem is visible, it tends to correlate with a slim leadership system that does not have enough glucose, enough weight, to stand up and ask strategic questions.

The exaggeration of an overweight managerial system leads to managerial pathological obesity, with 'managing the inevitable' being the main symptom (i.e. time is spent exclusively managing things that would happen anyway).

Oversized management on a diet, coupled with slim leadership eating healthier food and not skipping meals, sounds like a plan. There you are, the CEO as Chief Dietician Officer!

# PURPOSE IS THE NEW BLACK AND SOLIDARITY IS A BUILDING BLOCK

A combination of wisdom, moral compass and social doctrine from the Catholic Church, scattered through a series of documents over decades, never put together in a single volume, constitutes what is called Catholic Social Teaching. For many years, it has inspired religious and non-religious people, policy makers and leaders, spanning a great deal of the political and socio-economic spectrum. Even fierce detractors of the Catholic Church acknowledge the significant contribution that these documents have made to global Social Justice.

There are seven themes: Life and Dignity of the Human Person, Call to Family, Community and Participation, Rights and Responsibilities, Option for the Poor and Vulnerable, The Dignity of Work and the Rights of Workers, Solidarity and Care for God's Creation.

It was in this context that I was invited a while ago by a Catholic association to give a lecture presenting my views on Solidarity in the Workplace. The preparation for the talk made me think a lot and made me imagine what such a workplace could look like, beyond the nice words. I will share with you what I came up with; the 10 characteristics of a workplace were solidarity is alive:

1.  There will be a strong sense of interdependence. This is contrary to a culture of Social Darwinism where there is excessive internal competition. 'My safety is your safety' or 'my success is your success', for example, would be wonderful examples of this achievement.

2.  It will require a great deal of Social Intelligence: listening, putting oneself in other people's shoes. It is something organizations desperately need and that has become a topic of much conversation in recent years.

3. It will engender a sense of 'the collective'. Suddenly, questions such as 'who needs to know?' and the subsequent action and sharing, will make real sense.

4. It will spread a sense of accountability and responsibility. You need to know what you and others are responsible for in order to be able to contribute. Vagueness will not be supported.

5. It will also create awareness of the impact of my actions (of my work with others) on individual and collective commitments.

6. It will foster genuine cooperation, well beyond connectedness. Connectivity per se is not collaboration.

7. It will go far beyond a defensive attitude (I can be hurt, I am likely to be a victim) to reach the proactive 'we are all agents (of our destiny) here'.

8. It won't feel like 'theory' or just good works. It will be action (the word activism contains the word act).

9. It will require authentic leadership that supports all of the above.

10. It will generate trust. Vulnerability is OK: "*I won't be punished, we are all in this together.*"

My first reaction, during my own construction of the argument, surprised me in that this is not utopian. It's an aspiration for decent workplaces and fine organizations that have purpose and that enhance the individual.

In 2014, purpose is the new black. When in doubt, ask the new generations of workers and consumers. 'Solidarity thinking' may be a good glue for the Lego pieces of the modern remarkable organization.

# [50]

# COLLECTIVE LEADERSHIP: TWO ACID TESTS

Collective Leadership is what I call that state in the evolution of management teams or leadership teams where the power of the collective leadership is far greater than the sum of the power of the individual leaders, and where the team exercises leadership as a single unit, not as a collection of individuals. This is not the same as a 'high performance team', where the focus is on excellent coordination, collaboration and delivery. I see the 'high performance team' as a state of operational excellence, whilst I see 'Collective Leadership' as a state of unified, single drive.

I have two Acid Tests for this 'Collective Leadership'.

Number one is 'The Empty Chair Test'.

A member of the leadership team disappears for a period of time (prolonged illness, he is called away for a special project to acquire Company X, he is tasked with a sensitive corporate project that requires his full dedication, he is parachuted to a different location to sort out a serious crisis, he suddenly leaves, etc.) and his chair is empty. I am talking about either a functional chair (CFO, Head of HR, VP of IT, Head of R&D, etc.), or a Regional or P&L/Commercial chair (Head of Europe, MD of France, VP of EMEA, etc.). It does not matter. The answer to that empty chair situation is (1) that somebody else from the Leadership Team jumps in and says, "*I'll take care of your area/function*", and (2) and that this is not dictated by the CEO. It just happens.

For the latter, imagine your day-to-day family life (or somebody else's): "*The car needs petrol, I am late for work. OK, you take the other car, I'll take the kids to school and I'll get petrol.*" Describe to me, how many strategic committees were needed and how many discussions around 'my role-your role' took place before this decision was taken and actioned? Think about it, why is it that in organizations we are unable to replicate normal life? It's a mystery.

Acid test number two is 'The Wrong Members Town Hall'.

The Head of HR is visiting an affiliate at the same time as a scheduled local Town Hall meeting when all employees are gathered to hear some corporate news. Given this VIP visit, people would welcome an update on (1) New Product Launches and (2) overall Company Performance or Quarterly Results. But he is not a 'Commercial' person from HQ! However, the Head of HR (member of the Leadership Team) is still able to walk people through both. She has no commercial P&L responsibility, but as a member of the Leadership Teams she is able to deliver that speech, no problem. And people are a bit stunned, perplexed, amused and even surprised. Great!

Similarly, Peter, the Senior VP of Commercial Operations in Europe, Africa and the Middle East, finds himself unexpectedly in front of an annual event for HR people. Mary, the Head of HR has missed the plane for the Conference, but Peter, the commercial head of EMEA is in town. The audience is composed of the company-wide HR community and Peter is able to describe the entire HR strategic plan, no problem. And people are a bit stunned, perplexed, amused and even surprised. Great!

I am sure you get the message. But I have an equal number of clients saying that 'this is unrealistic' or that 'this is great and something to aspire to'.

In Collective Leadership mode, Functions, Regions, Support, P&L, non P&L, get blurred. Nobody expects people to be an expert in a functional, non-commercial area that is not theirs, but Collective Leadership means that it would be perfectly reasonable to deliver a non-expert, pretty accurate picture of any area, no matter what part of the business, if you are a member of the Leadership Team. Often a source of surprise, this solidarity is a hallmark of the power of Collective Leadership.

Imagine these two Acid Tests in your organization. Would it pass? Reflect on your own journey towards Collective Leadership. Whether you are at the top, or not quite at the top, or further away from the top: the principles apply.

If you are in the 'this is unrealistic' camp, my question to you is 'Why?'

# IT'S OFFICIAL: THE **MAGIC BULLET** THAT CHARACTERIZES GOOD LEADERSHIP IS TO BACK OFF!

It should not surprise us that people are constantly looking for the magic bullet of leadership. What makes a good leader? We are not short of answers. Reams of paper and servers full of gigabytes will give you any answer you wish. There is, for example, the typical list of values: integrity, courage, honesty, sensitivity, emotional and social intelligence, etc. The trouble is these lists of universal values are not very specific. They would apply equally well to being a good father, a good teacher or indeed to simply being a good human being.

I am sympathetic to the approach that asks a more refined question: "*What would it take to be a leader here, in company A, B, C?*" Still, you wish you could find the universal magic bullet, even if requires lots of translations and context.

But thanks to Google, we are a step closer to finding the bullet, or at least to understanding the potential magic. The data is interesting. It answers the question for Google and leaves us with a big hypothesis: could we extrapolate from this to our own non-Google-esque environments?

The reason why Google 'has the answer', is because a long time ago, Google decided to apply to their Human Resources the same rigour they applied to their engineering. That is, using data, something Google has in ample supply. Google is not shy to say that it is carrying out its own People Analytics all the time.

Consistently, through their internal analytics, Google finds that the single characteristic of the successful leader is predictability. Not very exciting, in fact, somewhat of an anti-climax at first reading. It means that people in Google feel that their (good) leaders are those who will not interfere or change their mind all the time. They will be consistent. That leads them to talk about the other side of the magic bullet: autonomy. Around these leaders, people feel that, within some parameters, they are free to act, make the most of themselves and be themselves. The predictable, consistent leader removes the main obstacle from the equation: himself. From here, it follows that another way they describe this singular characteristic of leadership is 'autonomy support'. Summary: the best Google leaders are consistent, therefore predictable. That gives autonomy to me, to make the best of me. They support my autonomy. Nice Human Algorithm.

The data is solid. No other parameters, from IQ to university grades or mental capacity correlate with 'good leadership'. I don't know how Google-esque we all are these days, but the 'Google evidence' is a clear reinforcement of the concept I have used formally since 2006: 'Backstage Leadership™'. It is the art of leaders giving the stage to others who can act. In the case of Viral Change™, the 'others' are those elected volunteers, highly connected and influent individuals within the organization who pioneer new behaviours. Beyond the Viral Change™ framework, they are subordinates, team members or other colleagues.

This idea is also consistent with an old obsession of mine: space. That is, that leadership should be concerned with the creation and protection of space both for themselves and for others (*The Leader with Seven Faces*, 2006). That this all closes the loop nicely on my own thinking is irrelevant here. What it does say, however, is that at the very least, this is a hypothesis worth testing in your own organization.

If, as I see it, a mature version of leadership is actually to back off as opposed to stepping in, then this has significant implications for leadership development. The single objection I get against my Backstage Leadership™ is people saying, "*If I do that, it will be a disaster, my people won't deliver.*" If this is the case, you have a problem. It's called you! Either you are in full command and control mode, so the problem is you, or you don't have the right people. If the latter, the problem is still you, unless you have inherited a colony of aliens.

# [52]

# THREE WAYS TO GET APPROVAL FROM YOUR CEO OR LEADERSHIP TEAM

Way number 1: My team has come up with these three options, A, B and C. Which one do you want us to do?

Way number 2: I need you to approve A. We also have options B and C, but we would not recommend them.

Way number 3: Just to let you know that we are doing A. We explored B and C, but they did not rank as high as A.

These 3 ways describe 3 different concepts of empowerment, 3 different styles of leadership and also 3 different organizations.

All 3 are legitimate, but they are very different. Don't kid yourself; they are not simple variations of the same thing.
Many people still ask for permission for things that the leadership does not expect to have to approve. But they may do so, because it's now on their plate, in front of them. Many Boards complain that decisions are 'pushed up' too much, but do very little to change the situation. On the other hand, many

leadership structures expect to be presented with options so they can make a final decision.

Knowing whether you are 1, 2 or 3 and, more importantly, whether you'd like to be 1 or 2 or 3, or which one of them your senior leadership expects, is fundamental. These questions are, more often than not, simply not posed or articulated. In these cases, decision making runs in automatic pilot mode, creating default positions that are never validated properly and that sooner or later, will drive people (top, middle or bottom) simply mad.

# TO BE A BETTER LEADER, TAKE A HOLIDAY FROM YOURSELF

The space of your Self is occupied. By you. This is good news and bad news. On the one hand, you are always with your Self. On the other hand, you may be too much with your Self. The Self can be your worst enemy, but could also be your best friend. Best friends occasionally irritate you, precisely because of their closeness, their proximity. Perhaps you have wished to take a little break from a 'best friend' from time to time.

Leaders need to be good friends with their selves. They need to have the insight and the maturity to see their Self in action: is it taking up too much space? Too little space?

There are times when you should take a holiday from 'yourself', as the late John O'Donohue would say. It does not have to be a long, exotic holiday, but can be more of a time-out or a break.

These are five sets of symptoms which may suggest that you should consider that holiday (soon):

1. You find yourself talking too much about yourself.
2. For the past little while you have been too harsh, perhaps too unkind, to yourself, blaming yourself for an unusual number of things.
3. You are missing some life-lines (not dead-lines) such as kids' birthdays, anniversaries or reunions. People seem to have that habit of having birthdays and anniversaries on the days you are travelling or absent.
4. You find yourself interfering too much in other people's lives, professional or personal.
5. You have not had a chance recently to ask yourself that question about 'what your legacy as a leader is', 'what kind of house you are building' or 'what you are leaving behind'.

There may be more symptoms, but these are pretty important. Trust me, I am a doctor.

Sure, to identify the symptoms, some insight capacity is required. Which I am assuming a leader has. If not, the case is terminal anyway.

You won't find these symptoms flagged in a traditional 'leadership manual'. This is part of the 'Not-Off-The-Shelf-Leadership-Stuff' Series.

# SPACE, TIME AND JOURNEYS

## SELLING TIME, PROTECTING SPACE, PATHS

# HEROES ON THE PAYROLL:
## THE GOOD NEWS AND THE BAD NEWS

Some people have a hero within. They have this tremendous ability to mobilize energy, jump in when big issues present themselves, work 24/7 on a peak project, do the extra-ordinary as if it were ordinary, go not just an extra mile or two, but the whole run, show amazing commitment and 'engagement', and achieve the unexpected. These are the corporate equivalent of a Hercules, Perseus, Achilles or Odysseus on the payroll. They write the epic narrative of the organization. Mini-mythology surrounds them. A mythology that may absorb the entire corporate narrative, based on just a couple of guys.

I have good news and bad news. The good news is that these 'heroes' create a sense of possibility. They show that making great efforts is something that happens inside the firm, that it's possible and they provide some glorious role models that may be very useful during more depressed times in the firm.

The bad news is that if people want to mirror their behavior and convert the company into an epic 24/7, permanent state of busy-ness (as opposed to business) and adopt heroic behavior as a prototype, we may end up with collective high adrenaline, which may or may not deliver good outcomes. The reason is illustrated in this story from the martial arts:

> A young boy travelled across Japan to study with a famous martial arts teacher. The master asked him what he wanted. The young boy told him he wanted to be the finest martial artist in the land and asked how long he had to study. *"Ten years at least"*, the master answered. *"But what if I studied twice as hard as all your other students?"* the young boy responded. *"Twenty years"*, the master replied. *"Twenty years! What if I practice day and night with all my effort?"* *"Thirty years"*, was the master's reply. The boy was thoroughly confused. *"How is it that each time I say I will work harder, you tell me that it will take longer?"*, the boy asked. The Master replied, *"The answer is clear. When one eye is fixed upon your destination, there is only one eye left with which to find the Way."* (Joe Hyams, *Zen in the Martial Arts*, 1982).

Extra-ordinary efforts may not always bring extra-ordinary results.

Organizations have a bad habit of rewarding efforts as opposed to rewarding outcomes. As with the young apprentice above, extra-ordinary, heroic efforts may confuse the mind, particularly the collective mind. Heroic role modeling on a grand scale is not a good way to run an organization. Or a School for Martial Arts, apparently.

# NO MILK, NO HONEY:

## ENJOY THE JOURNEY

Moses' leadership was bad. He promised his people a land of milk and honey. Instead, they got a terrible 40-year hike with no milk and no honey at the end. He would not be re-elected as CEO today (although he could probably still get a few million dollars on quitting).

The 'journey' and the 'travelling' are universal analogies. The hero's journey is an archetype for mankind. Perhaps nobody has put it better than Joseph Campbell (1904-1987) in his seminal *The Hero with a Thousand Faces* (1949).

There is 'journey leadership' and 'destination leadership'. 'Destination leadership' is OK if it's real and honest. But promise too much milk and honey and you may be in trouble. The problem with many 'destinations' is that they are like those holiday brochures that show a swimming pool in the compound, but not the construction work next door or the mosquitoes in the bathroom without hot water.

The ancient Greeks knew a thing or two about journeys. Odysseus lived on the Greek island of Ithaca and Homer wrote a whole epic poem about reaching this 'promised land', incidentally describing the island's features in a way that don't match the real island of Ithaca. But, who cares? The principle is the journey.

Constantine Cavafy's (1863-1933) poem *Ithaka* is required reading for my Leadership Programme. It describes the exciting prospect of reaching Ithaca, but soon warns that you should pay attention to every bit of the journey and *"hope the voyage is a long one, full of adventure, full of discovery."* And he recommends not hurrying the journey at all. *"Better if it lasts for years, so you are old by the time you reach the island, wealthy with all you have gained on the way, not expecting Ithaka to make you rich."*

We have a boring term for this in management: 'managing expectations'.

142

It warns you that Ithaca may even disappoint you, because after your *'marvelous journey'*, Ithaca may have *'nothing left to give you now'*. *"And if you find her poor, Ithaka won't have fooled you. Wise as you will have become, so full of experience, you will have understood by then what these Ithakas mean."*

Leadership may be, after all, the art of taking people on a journey to Ithaca, not the prescription of how to reach it.

It's the journey that matters, not the milk and honey.

# [56]

# A 6<sup>TH</sup> CENTURY LEADERSHIP MANUAL THAT STARTS WITH THE WORD: LISTEN!

It's impossible to listen in a noisy room. If you want to listen to your breathing, you need silence. You can't listen in busy-ness mode. We hear lots of things, but we listen to few.

Listening to music through your earphones when walking around is more hearing the music than listening to it.

We hear other people, we hear the CEO, we hear the news, we hear our team members, we hear complaints, we hear people suffering. It does not automatically follow that we listen to any of them. Listening is becoming a rare quality. It requires active willingness to do it.

There are four magic questions for leaders about listening:

(1) What am I saying?
(2) Am I being heard?
(3) Is anybody listening?
(4) How do I know any of the above?

# SPACE

In *The Leader with Seven Faces*, one of my books and the basis for my Leadership Programmes, language is face number one. The above questions are key leadership's hearing aids.

Listening is sometimes an anxious request: Listen to me! Would you please listen? One of the oldest Standard Operating Procedures (SOP) and Leadership Manuals in the world is The Rule of Saint Benedict, written in the 6th Century for monks in monasteries, although there were other similar Rules even before his. For centuries, it has inspired religious and non-religious life. It caters to all needs in the community and provides guidance and 'solutions' to potential problems. Even today, this Rule in its modern adaptation is in place in all Benedictine communities around the world. Benedict of Nursia, patron saint of Europe, wrote his Rule in ordinary Latin. It has a prologue and seventy-three chapters. Not bad for an SOP!

The Rule starts with one single Latin word: 'Ausculta', that is, Listen!

Perhaps he anticipated modern organizational life.

# [57]

# NEVER SELL YOUR TIME!

A friend of mine, a great artist, posted his latest challenge on Facebook. He had presented a product idea to his client. It was visually very simple and the copy was short. The client loved it and wanted to buy it, as he thought it would sell and make him lots of money. However, he then said that, because it was so simple and so clever, and despite the fact that it would sell perhaps better than a complex idea or complex artwork, he wouldn't pay my friend's usual rate because 'the artwork would take no time at all'. He wanted a huge price reduction. Naturally my friend had a stream of friends commenting on his post, full of sympathy and with lots of outrage, many comments approaching the limits of etiquette!

I felt very bad for my friend. Obviously, he was very troubled by this injustice. I rushed to post: *"Never sell your time. Nobody can afford it. Sell a product, an outcome, an idea. Not your time. Never your time! Declare your time unaffordable."*

Time is man's last asset. Sell your time and it will soon be depleted. It's a finite asset. As a consultant, I have professional fees, but not daily or hourly rates. I never charge per day or per hour. But I respect others who do so, from psychoanalysts and lawyers, to plumbers and locksmiths.

Executive search firms usually charge a percentage of the salary of the appointee. Private schools don't charge by the number of hours the kids are at school. Brand and advertising companies don't charge by the number of creative directors or principles or assistants involved, or the number of days taken until the concept is created.

In my consulting and speaking engagements, I provide value and I am paid for it. My advice, thought leadership, speech, consultation, collaboration, or hands-on project execution has a value and a fee. My time is unaffordable.

# [58]

# 'BED IN TEN MINUTES, YOU CAN PLAY TILL THEN' VERSUS 'YOU HAVE TEN MORE MINUTES TO PLAY BEFORE BED'

A little booklet on Behavioural Economics for kids gives this wonderful example on how the same ten minutes can be experienced in very different ways. The first option is a threat. The second has the joy of ten more wonderful extra minutes to play before bedtime. In both cases the kid has ten minutes. One has more chances than the other of ending in tears. Welcome to parental training in Behavioural Economics! OK, not quite!

This example falls under the so-called 'framing effect', something obvious, but often ignored. Another example of 'how we make choices' is this: what do you prefer, something that is advertised at 10 dollars, but comes with a cash discount of 50c? Or the 10 dollar item that is advertised at 9.50 dollars, but gives you the 50c credit on your credit card? In both cases, you pay 9.50 dollars, but people tend to feel much better with the first choice where there is a 'discount'.

There is a long list of 'effects' of this kind that Behavioural Economics, although it has not discovered them (they are well-entrenched in traditional Psychology), has managed to apply to day-to-day decision making, including investment decisions.

Framing is important in everyday life in organizations, not only in the decision-making arena, but also in the more generic area of the analysis of situations and conversations. The old adage *"We don't have problems, we have opportunities"* belongs here. It has been trivialized a lot, because it's over-used and has become management jargon. But it forms a very good basis from a behavioural perspective. Problem solving is a completely different occupation than opportunity building. Both examples here are looking at the same issue: 'ten minutes', 'ten dollars'.

Next time you <u>only</u> have two hours left to prepare your presentation and you have started panicking, remember that you <u>still</u> have two (wonderful) hours to prepare for that presentation. The second option will give you 'plenty of time.'

# [59]

# THE NEW UNITS OF SPACE AND TIME AND THE LATEST UPCOMING DISRUPTIVE INNOVATIONS

New units:

- Certificate of existence = 140 characters (Twitter).

- Presentation of ideas, maximum attention span = 18 min (TED).

- Digital reading, maximum attention space = 1 or 2 Smartphone screens max. (Not that long ago we used something called 'one page', as in, 'I'll send you a one page summary'. It was a unit in its own right. This is now a Smartphone screen with the exceptional allowance of a bit of scrolling down).

- Business time unit = the quarter

- A dialogue = a digital chat (WhatsApp, Facebook, Instagramm, Kik, Text message).

- Business reality: whatever can be fitted on a PowerPoint slide and bullet-pointed (as in this text, of course).

- A book page = a kindle screen.

- Busy-ness score = number of emails in my inbox.

- What your boss needs to know = Executive summary (most likely she will never read the 30 pages behind).

Strong upcoming Disruptive:

- The book (hardback is more innovation-disruptive).

- A physical letter (handwritten is even more disruptive; try to write one to your children, it's a perfect start).

- A face-to-face conversation (incredibly disruptive if held with a loved one and a bottle of wine, but also works with colleagues at work, loved or not).

- A briefing document without Executive Summary.

- Presentation without slides (this disruptive innovation has been in the making for years, but it has not quite made it yet).

- Bookshop and library browsing.

- Silence (included in my 'Border Diet').

- Banning the word 'basically' at the start of a sentence.

(Sorry, I am running out of screen…)

# 'PATHS, NOT WORKS'.

## A PHILOSOPHER'S METAPHOR THAT EXPLAINS OUR LEADERSHIP CHALLENGES

The philosopher Martin Heidegger (1889-1976), requested before his death that the collection of his writings be called 'Paths, not works'. He had used the word 'paths' several times. According to some interpreters of his works, it provides an image of 'leading', but not necessarily to anywhere in particular; like many paths do in the woods.

Good leaders are good path-makers. Sometimes the journey is not clear. The destination may still be ambiguous. It's the journey, stupid! Pretending that there is a fixed destination and that you know all the highways, roads and pathways, does not make you a good or better leader.

The great Spanish poet Antonio Machado (1875-1939) said it well in one of his most acclaimed poems. In English, it would read something like this: *"Walker, there is no path to follow, you make the path by walking."*

The allegory of the Path, whether Machado's path-making or Heidegger's 'paths, not works', is a good allegory for leadership. I have spoken before of the leader as a Cartographer, as a map-maker (*New Leaders Wanted,* 2007).

The pilgrimage is also a good metaphor for a leadership journey, an ever reflective journey, made not in solitude, but accompanied by followers. Not surprisingly, the image of the Journey is also frequently associated with leadership. The Journey contains all sorts of challenges and discoveries for the pilgrim, as it does for the leader.

All this is crucial to a form of 'leadership thinking' in short supply: the reflective one, the emergent, the discoverable, the non-prescriptive. I make no secrets of my mistrust of 'a set of characteristics' or 'a list of attributes' for the good leader. Yet, I understand those 'sets' (very often of dubious evidence-based origin) as maps. I respect the maps, but not when they become an end in their own right.

I am in favour of any path, any Journey that prompts questions. Questions such as 'what does it mean to be a leader here?' or

**153**

'why would anybody come with me on this journey where we are going to make the path by walking?'

I am worried about our natural ability to provide answers even without the questions. Off-the-shelf leadership development is not healthy. It is finished works, not paths in the making.

SPACE

[61]

# LOOKING AT A SCREEN IS THE NEW NORMAL

There was this big conference that was introduced by the chairman in this way: "*Welcome everybody. Lovely to have you all here; now we can all look at our screens together.*" There was a time when people took notes at conferences; now people tweet whilst 'listening'. Why? Because they can.

It's quite normal now at conferences to have a twitter feed displayed on a large screen next to the main presentation, so people can see and read the instant reaction of the audience to what the presenter is saying in 'real time'. Why do we do this? Because we can.

In smaller meetings, it used to be considered rude to have your laptop on and 'do emails' whilst somebody was presenting. It was rude, but tolerated. Now there are less laptops on the table, but people are looking down at their Blackberries and Smartphones. 'Homo Erectus' is being replaced by 'Homo Thumbing', which is an illuminated Homo-Looking-Down!
I have run client meetings with apocalyptic warnings against doing this and descriptions upfront of the consequences if not adhered to (from being publicly put on the spot by me, including CEOs; to paying a nominal fine or even to buying the

beers in the evening). Everybody complies at the beginning. By the end of the first day, trespassers are apparent. By the second day, everybody ignores the warning and looks down again, thumbing with an apparent vengeance.

There is an issue here of etiquette, politeness and respect that is big enough. But even bigger is the issue of busy-ness and the apparent inevitability of having to answer a trivial message on the spot. Our hyper-connected world has given us enormous possibilities, but also a new Ego Archetype that reads like this: "*What we say, surely, must be incredibly important for many people; to say it immediately is paramount, and if we don't live in instant reaction mode, instant thinking, instant presence, instant action, there is something wrong with us.*" Why do we react and reply at the command of a beep of the Smartphone? Because we can.

Human interaction is being digitally re-defined every single day in millions of places. I don't have a good answer, but my question is: What are we, human beings, losing? I know it may be a naïve question, but 'the new normal' bothers me.

# IT'S PERSONAL

AUTHENTICITY,
PERMISSION TO BE HUMAN
THE THINGS YOU DON'T
HAVE TO SAY,
WALLS

# YOU WANT TO SEEK THE COMPANY OF A FEW REJECTED PEOPLE

There are many compilations of famous rejected people, but I found these examples on distractify.com. These are cases of rejection that should make us think twice about giving up in adversity.

Some are better known than others:

Walt Disney was fired from a paper because he 'lacked imagination and had no good ideas'.

JK Rowling suffered dozens of rejections, including Harper Collins, before somebody considered publishing Harry Potter.

Oprah Winfrey was fired as an evening news reporter because she mixed in too many emotions in her stories.

George Orwell was told that it was impossible to sell animal stories in the USA. So they did not publish Animal Farm.

Elvis Presley was told by a manager that he was better off sticking to his previous job of driving trucks in Memphis.

Steve Jobs was fired from Apple. He was asked to go back, of course!

Stephen King's wife saved the manuscript for Carrie, which had been rejected thirty times and was in his trash.

Marilyn Monroe was told she should consider becoming a secretary instead of a model.

Abraham Lincoln, and I quote the entire sentence here: "was *demoted from Captain to Private during the war, failed as a businessman, and lost several times as a political candidate before becoming President*".

Madonna was also rejected, Andy Warhol was rejected by the Museum of Modern Art in New York, U2 was rejected by a record company, Sylvia Plath was requested to cut half of *Amnesiac* by The New Yorker and there are so many more...

If you've been rejected because of your imagination, rest assured, you are in good company!

# AUTHENTICALLY DISRUPTIVE

Pope Francis has introduced disruption. The head of the 1.2 billion strong Catholic Church lives in a one bedroom apart-hotel, produces off-the-cuff daily comments, does not speak English and gets really angry with the retiring top Vatican Official who has arranged a nice penthouse for him. In 2013, he drew three times the number of visitors to his audiences, compared with his predecessor.

In Israel, he breaks with protocol (and security) and prays not just at the Western Wall in Jerusalem, the holiest prayer site in Judaism, but also at the other wall: the not so holy separation wall that divides Israel and Palestine. He ends up inviting the Israeli and Palestinian Prime Ministers to the Vatican, not for peace talks (*"that would be crazy on my part"*, he says), but to pray together, at his place.

He has managed to appear on the cover of Time magazine, but also in a prominent gay magazine as 'Person of the Year'. Graffiti on the walls of Rome picture him as a flying Superman in white robes.
The English version of his first Letter to the Faithful, which is the length of a manifesto pamphlet and does not even bear the rank of Encyclical (the recognized, 'official' pastoral document), has sold more copies than the entire collection of

Encyclicals of all previous Popes (to the delight of the ailing British publisher).

He drives the conservative arm of the Catholic Church completely nuts, because Popes are supposed to be very careful about what they say and they are expected to use a deep theological language, not speak like your local priest during his Sunday service. The liberals don't know what to make of him either because he is not going 'as far as they expected'. Atheists say that he is somebody worth talking to and they call him 'awesome' in their twitter feeds. The Cynical, a category in abundance thanks to the modern predominance of spin and the erosion of trust in politicians and public figures in general, say that 'surely, he must be a fake'.

I have two hypotheses. Number one: he is all spin; a calculated media-manipulator, Machiavellian extraordinaire, a great salesman, a natural PR guy. This is what some people say. The trouble with this hypothesis is that spin, as we know it, as practiced by politicians and public figures, needs good PR machinery behind it. The Vatican has the worst PR system on the planet. The Vatican's Head of Communications, a fellow Jesuit, sometimes seems to be the last one to know what the Pope plans to say. So either Pope Francis has supernatural and divine PR skills, in which case he is de facto a One-Man-Spin-Band – a very unlikely scenario - or this hypothesis simply does not hold water.

Hypothesis number two. The man is authentic. He speaks and acts according to what he thinks and believes. What you see and hear is him! And because he is 100% 'The Real Thing', this turns out to be very disruptive! Authenticity is disruptive because our expectations are so low. In a fake world, the authentic is unexpected and sometimes troublemaking. The true disruptive idea is Being Oneself.

I believe that in Leadership, authenticity wins the battle hands down. It may be hard to believe, but the truthful, the genuine,

162

the authentic, the honest and the humble have an advantage in today's world. In organizations, having the courage to be oneself, not the corporate man, not the yes-man, not the no-man, not the fake citizen, but just oneself, may be the kind of disruption we need. Leaders in business could do with disposing of their uniforms, their costumes, their layers of protective social makeup and their masks and try the Francis way. Who knows, that may well take care of a lot of the leadership development that we think is needed.

# [64]

## THE THINGS YOU DO NOT HAVE TO SAY, MAKE YOU RICH

William Stafford's (1914 - 1993) poem reads:

*"The things you do not have to say make you rich,*
*Saying the things you do not have to say weakens your talk.*
*Hearing the things you do not have to hear dulls your hearing,*
*And the things you know before you hear them; these are you*
*and the reason you are in the world."*

Attention leaders! Judging from the above, we are pretty poor. We talk too much, we command too much, we say too much, we repeat. I am not against the famous 'walk the talk'. It's just that I think the order is wrong. This proposes to walk first and then do the talking about the walk: but why walk? What are the benefits of the walk, why should others join the walk? Talk the walk! If people see you walking, maybe then you will have less to say. And, if as a leader, you accumulate more and more things that you don't have to say, you are rich, and you are doing great as leader.

This is lesson One of Disruptive Economics for Leadership:
The things you don't have to say make you a rich leader.

# STOP PRESS: CANDIDATE INTERVIEWED BY AUTHENTIC PEOPLE!

A recent senior hire in a client company commented to me that the thing that most impressed her in the round of interviews was that everybody seemed to be themselves. She had the perception that nobody was trying to project a particular 'party line', or was acting differently from how they really were. Some were very nice, others less. It was, paraphrasing the candidate, an invitation to be oneself in that particular company. There was something fresh and appealing about it. And so she joined.

I had a similar experience many years ago when working for a big multinational. The HQ environment was stiff, corporatized. It was a cloning machine, with its own dialect, a language not spoken outside those walls by any other human being. Headhunted to another company, I went for the standard round of interviews. Regardless of the content related to the job in question, I thought: "*Oh God, these people actually speak and act normally.*" It was refreshing. I joined.

Authenticity is precious, but it is often difficult to describe. However, when you see it, you know it. The great sociologist Erving Goffman (1922-1982), using comparisons from the world of theatre, wrote about how we try to control human interaction in *The Presentation of Self in Everyday Life* (1959). Our personas are our own versions of the Self and they may vary. However, authenticity beats any artificial persona, and certainly always wins over the 'corporate persona'.

After all, 'Authentic' comes from autos (self) and hentes (doer and being). Fake it and you'll be found out.

# HEAVEN IS EMPTY OF SELF-CENTRED PEOPLE

These were recent words of Pope Francis to the Italian bishops, apparently too preoccupied with their own careers and favours in the Vatican.

These are also words of wisdom for leadership. Leadership and self-centered attitudes do not go well together. Self-centered leaders are bad leaders, dangerous leaders. Leadership requires a servant attitude and this is incompatible with a self-centered focus. In fact, a re-focusing of 'the centre' may even be a requisite for success.

There was a moment in the 2008 Obama campaign when the grassroots movement began to be organized. Almost in passing, David Plouffe, campaign manager at the time, later wrote in his book *The Audacity to Win: The Inside Story and Lessons of Barack Obama's Historic Victory (2009)* that the message to the grassroots was: "*It's not about him, it's about you*!" Obama was very good at re-focusing attention from himself to the issues and to the activists.

Self-centered leadership is an oxymoron and a dangerous one at that. The good news is that these pseudo-leaders are very visible from a distance. My advice: avoid them like the plague, because whatever they pretend to lead, the focus is most likely on themselves and not on the real issues of concern.

# BUT I NEVER HEARD THE BUILDERS!

There is an 'Accidental Literature for Leaders'. This is what I call my compilation of poems or pieces of narrative that are not intended for management education (!), but serve us well for reflection. They are cheaper than a leadership development programme too!

This is a beautiful poem from Constantine P. Cavafy (1863 – 1933), a Greek poet with a day job as a journalist and civil servant. Which gives hope to everyone with a day job...

## Walls
*With no consideration, no pity, no shame,*
*they have built walls around me, thick and high.*
*And now I sit here feeling hopeless.*
*I can't think of anything else: this fate gnaws my mind—*
*because I had so much to do outside.*
*When they were building the walls, how could I not have noticed!*
*But I never heard the builders, not a sound.*
*Imperceptibly they have closed me off from the outside world.*

## Leader's action plan:
Make sure that you hear the builders.
Make sure that your people hear the builders.
Look out for walls around you that appear out of nowhere.
Make sure you are not building walls for your people.
If it looks like a wall, make sure you can open a door or a window.
If inevitable, chose your own walls.
If it's too late, at least paint the walls.
Tell your children about builders who build walls and make no noise.

[68]

# CHOOSING WHAT WE LOSE

*"We've lost money, we've lost nothing.*
*We've lost honour; we've lost a lot.*
*We've lost confidence, we've lost everything."*

This old saying is about choosing wisely. Choosing what to lose, that's it.

It brings to mind the central question of trust and confidence. Underestimated in our time, to lose trust is in many ways irreparable. You can never really get back to where you were. There is a breach. The line has been crossed, often only realized when it's too late. It's done. Confidence is lost.

Choices, choices.
Especially when it comes to what to lose.

# [69]

# WHEN IN DOUBT, MAKE IT PERSONAL

Invited to present at TEDx East London, I had lots of conversations with its wonderful curator, Maryam Pasha. The theme of the TEDx was 'Society Beyond Borders'. I had a flow of ideas about how the digital world has forced a redefinition of borders and the consequent paradoxes: the end of space and time that does not increase our proximity; hyper-connectivity that does not make us hyper-collaborative, etc.

I had a clear idea of the first part of the talk. What was less clear to me was 'Part 2' or the 'So what?' Like those TV contests, some movies and some video games, I had two possible endings for the script. I could easily go for the logical 'commercial' side. After all, my consulting work has to do with large-scale behavioural change and we use the power of peer-to-peer influence as a currency. We know about networks and human connectivity. This is natural territory for me. Or I could perhaps go for a more personal side: the liabilities of lack of borders for the Self and the Soul in the new digital world. In praising 'no borders' ('Anything without Borders' has a head start), we have forgotten the dangers of the Full Disclosure of The Self that many people seem so comfortable with.

# IT'S PERSONAL

Option A's end was clear, but Option B's ending was fuzzy, more of a nagging problem in my head: adolescents living in that world of Full Disclosure, the relinquishing of privacy, the cult of transparency, identity in cyberspace, etc. My old psychiatrist hat was nagging me too much to let me avoid these themes...

I did offer Maryam both Option A and Option B, quite convinced that A (the logical, commercial, well-crafted version) would win. I was wrong. In her gentle, but firm curatorship, I was directed towards the corridor of my unfinished thoughts. *"Make it personal"*, she said. The same week I had a chat with a business partner and I shared with him my dilemma. He asked me straight out: *"Where is your heart?"* I confessed my heart belonged firmly to B. *"Well, it's a no-brainer then. That would be You talking!"*

Yes, personal wins. Personal won on the day too. It was good advice for when in doubt. I should have known ... but I needed a good curator and a good business partner to point me at the more difficult and less obvious option. Authenticity works.

# [70]

# PERMISSION
# TO BE HUMAN

I have had a brilliant two-day meeting with a brilliant client. One aspect of my work with organizations that I truly enjoy is to help craft the 'Behavioural DNA' that shapes the culture of the company. This is a set of actionable behaviours that must be universal within the organization, from the CEO to the MRO (Mail Room Officer). They also need to pass the 'new hire test': would you put that list in front of a prospective employee and say 'This is us'?

There was one 'aspirational' sentence that I put to the test: 'Working here makes us better human beings'.

It was met with skepticism by the large group in the meeting, initially mainly manifested only through body language, including the difficult to describe cynical smiles. The rationalists in the group then jumped in to 'corporatize' the sentence. *"Do you mean better professionals?"* The long discussion had started. The full-blown corporate Academy of Language – from anything to do with skills, talent management, empowerment to being better managers, being better leaders, and so on, was brought to the table.

*"No, I mean better human beings. Period!"* I pushed back. Silence.

Next stage was the litany of adjectives to describe their discomfort, coming from the collective mental thesaurus: fluffy, fuzzy, soft and vague…

I felt compelled to reframe the question: *"OK, so who is against working in a place that makes you inhuman? Everybody. OK. So who is against working in a place that makes you more human? Nobody."* But still, the defensive smiling persisted.

It went on for a while until the group 'organically', by the collective hearing of pros and cons, turned 180 degrees until everybody agreed that 'Working in a place that makes you a better human being' was actually very neat. But - there was a but - *"Our leadership team won't like it. They will say that it's fluffy, fuzzy, soft, etc…"* In the words of the group, it was not them anymore who had a problem; it was the infamous 'they'.

I then continued to push back: *"Let's test it then."* There was a joint meeting with the top leadership team scheduled for later in the day. The statement 'Working here makes us better human beings' was, amongst others, up for discussion. The leadership team loved it, each and every one of them. Permission granted. Now we could relax and safely say that 'Working here makes us better human beings.' It's funny how our corporate uniforms make us feel uncomfortable with humanity, as if this is beyond the scope of work, outside of the job description, in need of top approval. *"Excuse me, can we say 'human' here?"* *"Yes, you can."* Thanks!

# STRATEGY
## NOT EVEN WRONG
## STRATEGIC OPTIONS
## SURPRISE,
## COMPETITORS

# WRITE A SCRIPT, NOT A STRATEGIC PLAN

A year from now, you all are here standing in front of the CEO saying: we screwed up! Write the script for that year and what happened to take you there.

A year from now, you all are here standing in front of the CEO saying: we succeeded! Write the script for that year and what happened to take you there.

Very often I run these exercises ('Success and Failure Scenarios') with parallel sub-teams of Boards, top leadership teams or management teams. I ask them to literally write those scripts down, or at least find all the pieces and assemble them in the same way as a script constructed for a novel, film or short story. People are incredibly good at writing these scripts (the failure scenario is invariably faster...) and can relate to them much better than to an account of goals and targets as written in the Strategic Plan. The storyteller inside of us seems to enjoy the questions and the production of answers.

For a long time now in my work, I have switched focus from 'Mission & Visions' to 'Space in the World' and 'Compelling narrative'. This is not a simple change of terms. The questions are different. The emphasis is on 'What do you want to be remembered for?' and 'What's the story, your story, perhaps your unique story?'

I also insist on writing down the headlines my clients would like to see in the newspapers in year one, or two, or within a relevant time frame. A couple of lines, that's all. I have seen more executives surprise each other in this exercise than in many other interactions. These visual narratives are very powerful. They bring the authentic part of us to the surface.

Another method I use is to ask people to answer (again, all in writing) a question posed by their children (or other children if they don't have children of their own): "*Dad/Mum/Sir, what do you do, exactly?*" The exercise always starts with some light jokes until it gets really serious. Try to articulate 'maximize shareholder value' to your 5-year old!

It's scripts, narratives, stories; not targets, numbers or earnings per share. There is nothing intrinsically wrong with targets, numbers and earnings per share, but the signposts are not places in their own right.

If you care about the journey and the place, you need a story. If you have a good, compelling one, there will be lots of good people who will choose to travel with you.

# "GOD, MAKE ME CHASTE, BUT NOT YET"

Augustine of Hippo, Saint Augustine in the Christian world, was very specific in his plea. He had a good idea of the destination, but wanted to postpone the journey a little. We have many Augustines in our organizations. Here are some management statements of the Augustine type:

We need to switch from product-centric to customer-centric. But not yet! Products are selling nicely (and we love customers anyway) so we'll get there someday. Soon.

We need to change this performance management system that has been in place for many years and that everybody hates. But not yet! It does the trick and we have spent a lot of time and money on it.

We really need to tackle culture. But not yet! Let's have all the people and processes and all the pieces in place first. First things first. Culture comes later. And it's going to be long and difficult. And I am not sure what it means, anyway.

We need to review our structure, which has become a bit of a monster. But not yet! Maybe it's not that bad and I can't even begin to face the hassle that this will involve.

We really need to address the behaviour of those Super-Salesmen we have who are so incredibly arrogant and toxic to our teams. But not yet! They are bringing in good revenues month after month. We'll do it at a later stage.

We need to address our overweight executive compensation and bonus system that is veering towards the un-ethical. But not yet! Stakeholders here have not made any noise and we would be upsetting so many high fliers.

We need to tackle our Global Ethics so that our business practices in the Third World are in line with our corporate values. But not yet! There are no complaints of misconduct. Nothing is broken and we need to be a bit flexible with Developing Countries. Cultures are different.

We need to look deeper into the behaviours of our guys on the trading floor. But not yet! Some of them are incredibly creative and worth a fortune. They will go somewhere else anyway. Besides, try to justify that to my boss.

We need to do lots of uncomfortable things to deal with questionable practices. But not yet! Because nothing is broken and we are making the numbers quarter after quarter.
The Jewish religious leader Hillel the Elder (around 10AD), said in *Ethics of the Fathers*:

*"If I am not for myself, who is for me? And if I am only for myself, what am I? And if not now, when?"* He is the real father of 'And if not now, then when?'

Many people in our modern organizations may say: *"First of all, Mr Hillel, you have too many questions. But to answer your last one, the answer is 'Not Yet'!"*

LIST YOUR **COMPETITORS,** THEN COMPARE YOURSELF WITH SOMEBODY **NOT ON THAT LIST**

I know this is not how it is supposed to work. But nothing about how things are supposed to work prepares us for how today's business actually works. In the past, businesses have grown by looking sideways. If you were Glaxo, you looked at Merck; if you were BP, you looked at Shell; if you were Avis, you looked at Hertz. Whoever you were, you looked at your competitors. There was always a handy list of them, and there were always companies ready to sell you benchmark data to ensure you that your sideways vision was in focus.

Benchmarking (which, many years ago, I called 'A race against somebody who had already won') created a phenomenon called 'Mr Above Average', which represented a kind of comfort zone that would allow you to sleep well. And sleep well we did.

Today, looking sideways at your competitors misses the point. If you keep doing so, you are bound to look, feel and smell like them. Perhaps better than such and such, but mostly like them. Your mind is bound to copy them even in structural terms: a sales force, a social media strategy, centralized services. And then what? Is that it? Well, you may earn the incredible prestigious label of The Next Kodak.

To seriously succeed and seriously create a legacy in our times, your comparisons need to be with companies outside of that list of 'natural competitors'. The answers, the imitations, the inspirations, the mirrors, the aha- moments, the drivers and the aspirations all lie somewhere else: in other sectors, other industries, other geographies, other models. It is an incredibly creative exercise and more than just a bit audacious. It's also fun.

This rule is applicable whether you are a multinational, a medium-sized company, a local one, a professional services firm or a one-man band consultant. Looking sideways is the temptation, but looking up and down and anywhere else is the path to being remarkable.

# STRATEGY

The competitive advantage lies not in trying to gain advantage over your competitors. Although I dislike grandiose and predictable examples, I am compelled to say that Apple did not look at Sony or Dell and Amazon did not look at Barns and Noble. However, Nike, Adidas, Puma and Reebok still look at each other, sideways. Hilton, Marriott, and Hyatt still look at each other, sideways. Get the picture?

# [74]

# BIOGRAPHY
# OF A FLIPCHART

A meeting room without a flipchart is like decaffeinated coffee. The absence of a flipchart insinuates possibly lots of talking, perhaps a conference or video call, but not necessarily the rolling up of sleeves and 'working on something'. The flipchart implies brainstorming, getting things out in the open, a license to throw up ideas and the possibility of capturing them.

Ah! Capturing! And these ideas will be held captive once they are on the flipchart. Eventually complex thoughts will be deconstructed into bullet points. Bullet points will grow in numbers and a second sheet will be required. Perhaps a third. And then, something magic will happen in all those brains in the room. Magic, because for some reason they all of a sudden all think in sync: Prioritize! Prioritization is merciless murder. 'We need to get it down to the three key items' or five if we are feeling generous.

(I sometimes have this mental picture of people waiting for Moses to come down from the mountain with The Tablet announcing: *"I've got 10 commandments"* and the Jews shouting back, *"Prioritize! Give us the top three!"*)

By now, flipchart sheets will be used as wallpaper. People feel good with all these white paper sheets around, full of colours, letters, circles, arrows, bullet points... It means productivity, offspring, worth, capacity, good brains, progress. Occasionally, an extra-terrestrial invasion of yellow post-its land on the flipcharts by the hand and command of the Categorization Squad. The take-over converts the multi-coloured sheets into tall, white buildings with lots of little yellow windows. The room becomes a city full of buildings of the same size, all next to each other. The meeting room is now a Disney-coloured supermarket of captive ideas.

But now it's time to debrief, to stand up and tell the story of what the flipchart says. Perhaps one of the sheets survives and will be taken away in a briefcase to new territories, uncomfortably folded for traveling. For the rest, left behind, death is approaching. Prolonged agony at first, then they will remain piled together, one on top of the other, perhaps for months. All mixed up. Those financial projection sheets lying together with the sheets full of circles and arrows from the previous session with the marketing visitors, and these themselves beneath a sheet from an obscure brainstorming session on where to build a plant. And all of these sheets rest on top of a list of pristinely described, never achieved, completely forgotten meeting objectives.

The flipchart is the largest corporate graveyard of ideas. Their individual biographies are the Lost Scrolls of corporate memory.

# NOT EVEN WRONG

Consistently attributed to physicist Wolfgang Pauli, who had no time for sloppy thinking, 'not even wrong' has become a category in its own right. It's not bad thinking, it's not even wrong! I love the concept and I love the extension of the spectrum, good to bad. I suppose at the other extreme, there is the 'beyond extraordinarily good'.

Somehow, good to bad was just too small a distance for Pauli. His impatience gave us the freedom to call something that is truly bad not even wrong. And 'not even wrong' means it's not even worth saying how bad it is.

It would be healthy to be able to say that some hypotheses about human behaviour or some assumptions about employee engagement, or an approach to leadership are 'not even wrong'. Clarity, honesty, candour are qualities in short supply in day-to-day management.

The other extreme would also be fantastic. Imagine the categories 'astoundingly exceptional', 'beyond brilliant' or 'incredibly awesome'.

But 'remarkable' does it for me. With my team we are in the business of building remarkable organizations.

Business language does not like hyperboles, but we need some of them to deal with the rather dull business idiom. I welcome the stretch at both extremes: from 'not even wrong' to 'out of this world'. Let's experiment with this thinking.

Acknowledgement: this was inspired by my son, Tom, who often refers to my jokes as 'not even funny'!

# [76]

# 10 STRATEGIC OPTIONS

These are the 10 strategic options you have at your disposal all the time, as I use them with my clients:

Options:

1. Change the oil (continuous improvement).

2. Let's use less oil (management of the 'denominator', efficiency).

3. But what kind of oil? ('in-the-box' thinking).

4. It's the wrong car! ('in-the-box' redirection).

5. We don't need a car/'it's transport, stupid!' (disruptive).

6. Too many cars, no drivers! (dysfunctional to functional, reconfiguration).

7. Ferrari? Ford? Bicycle? Walk? (disruptive, 'out-of-the-box').

8. Cars–R–us, Transport–R–us; Something–R–us (excellence).

9.  Let's transform the way cars are made (reboot!)

10. Let's make a dent in the universe (Steve Jobs, place in the world).

The question is not whether one is better than the other. It's a choice. If you just want to change the oil in the car, fine, but then don't expect innovation. The serious problem here is how we fool ourselves. Sometimes we come to believe that we are in sophisticated strategic mode, when all we are really doing is reshuffling the configuration of the company. Ah! But don't forget the experts used in sourcing the oil, tendering for the most effective oil and the competitor analyses of the different kinds of oil used by competitors.

When I use this model with my clients, it becomes very apparent what the client is trying to do. Straight away, it deals with a common trap that people very often find themselves falling into: "*I think we all agree, we are just saying the same thing differently.*" No, we are not! Don't ever believe that people 'are saying the same thing differently'. Certainly not in strategic terms.

# MAXIMIZING, OPTIMIZING, SATISFICING

These three things are different. They represent three forms of decision making, but I suggest they also represent three different kinds of people. Call it personality, or genetic predisposition, or both. It's important to understand these differences because in our organizations we have a mixture of the three. You as manager or leader would fall into one of these categories. Ignoring the differences between them has a price, mostly in the form of driving each other mad.

'Driving each other mad' is a main feature of teams (top or otherwise), or any other form of social grouping, especially when people do not understand the impact of differences in 'work preferences' or their different mental frames on decision making. Labelling it 'we have a communication problem' doesn't help because it doesn't mean anything. In fact, most 'communication problems' have little to do with communication and so much more with differences in 'zones of comfort'. Decision making is one of these zones.

Maximizing implies making the most of the utility of things. Optimizing means obtaining the best possible outcome from what is available. These two approaches are easy to understand although again and again, you will see people confusing one with the other.

Far less entrenched in language is the concept of satisficing: declaring something as 'enough' once found amongst a number of alternatives. Satisficing is an old concept defined by Herbert A. Simon (psychologist, sociologist, economist) in 1956 to explain the behaviour of decision makers under circumstances in which an optimal solution cannot be determined.

The good maximizer needs to know and explore all possibilities in order to decide what the maximum benefit is. The optimizer will choose 'the best possible outcome' as a priority, and this may not be the maximum. The satisficer will shortcut quite a lot of the exploration and will make a decision once an acceptable threshold of 'good' or 'desired' has been found. I repeat, this is done at the expense of not looking at all possibilities and therefore, potentially missing something much better. It's not that the satisficer settles for just anything, but that his mind does a mental calculation: Is the cost of exploring all possibilities in order to maximize or optimize the choice worth the effort, or is this good enough to decide, move on and spend that energy somewhere else?

Let's say we go shopping. I need to buy a new suit. The big shopping mall has at least 10 places where I can buy a suit, but I don't know them particularly well, so I can't go straight to the one that I like and know that I should buy from. I start from the South and move up. I hit the first suit shop. I don't like what I see. I keep moving and find the second. Here, there is a decent suit, good price and very acceptable for what I need. I like it. The maximizer would ask them to keep it for him, and he will continue to visit the other eight shops until he has all the data to make a decision, which will be based upon the best value for money. The optimizer will do the same, but may buy the best, in his judgment (and concept of 'optimum') even if not the cheapest. Both will need to know what all the possibilities are, so both will visit the entire mall. The satisficer buys the suit in shop 2 and spends the time that it would have taken to visit the rest of the mall, doing something else. His mind has asked the question: "*Is it really worth spending three more hours here if the suit I have in front of me is great?*" And he also says: "*Get out, go home and finish your book before you get trapped in rush hour traffic.*"

The maximizer and optimizer think that the satisficer is lazy, or has bad judgment, or does not care much about suits other than getting one. The satisficer finds the others tedious, obsessive and trying to rationalize something (decision making for suits) that does not deserve this level of rationalization.

The above are, of course, caricatures. However, if you as a leader are trying to understand your people in terms of the mental models they are using for decision making, you are well

194

on your way to avoid conflicts by not simply reverting to labelling them 'communication problems'.

Notes to self:

Note 1: maximization and optimization are politically correct options in organizations.

Note 2: try to assess yourself against these criteria without using 'it depends' at the start of your sentence.

Note 3: you may think that you are a satisficer when buying suits and optimizer when writing a strategic plan. If so, imagine a strategic plan written with the satisficer 'decision-making hat'. You may discover some major benefits.

# [78]

# THE PLACE CALLED ROW (REST OF THE WORLD)

In the old days, when I worked for an American company, our business was split between the USA and the Rest of The World, which we called ROW. I belonged to ROW. And the citizens of ROW were clearly not of the same league. It was not just my company who used the ROW concept, it was quite common.

Things are more sophisticated nowadays, but we still make distinctions: emergent markets, developing countries, developed or mature markets, etc. Regional structures are also in place and a new form of ROW is for instance EMEA. This, of course, stands for Europe, Middle East and Africa, a sort of grouping which most often is united by geographical proximity on a world map in the Executive Suite, and little else.

Being an ROW-ite or an EMEA-ite, or more often, an Emergent Market citizen is not necessarily bad. As Emergent Markets, the assumption is that you are behind those who have already emerged, so you need to catch up. I personally prefer to see this as an opportunity to avoid the mistakes of the Emerged and Mature and to 'jump the curve'. I have worked with clients in the past who have told me: "*We are just like Germany (or Italy or France), only 10 years behind."* What a wonderful opportunity to avoid 10 years of mistakes! (Unless you are blind and want to repeat them.)

Jumping the curve, avoiding the pain of mistakes, accelerating growth in its own right without having to go through the same process as others have gone through before, is smart. It can be done. Entire Industrial Revolutions have been bypassed. When in doubt, look at Ireland.

If you have a Corporate ROW passport, you may be luckier than you think!

# [79]

# SURPRISE!

Surprise is a powerful strategy in its own right. Surprise means being ahead of the game, being further ahead than others thought you would be, being able to pull an organizational solution out of your hat, disclose the next new idea when nobody was expecting one, take a rabbit out of the hat or bring to the market something that nobody has asked for.

Surprise the market, surprise your boss, surprise yourself, surprise your followers, surprise your teams, surprise the guys in corporate. Or all of the above.

I know what you are thinking. Your boss does not like surprises. In fact, there are two types of bosses who don't want surprises. Type one: The ones who don't want bad surprises. Type two: the ones who don't want any surprise at all, good or bad. Type one is understood; nobody wants bad news. You would not set out to surprise with bad news. Not on purpose at least! The latter is a tricky one, because there are many people who, in fact, hate unpredictability. For them 'meeting the budget' is better than being surprised with savings. In other words, predictable numbers are better than unpredictable ones, even if these are better numbers. If you head up a cost centre, such as R&D, spending every penny or cent may be 'better' than producing 'an under-spend'. I've seen people labeled as bad managers due to their not having spent what they said they would. If you don't understand this, you may not have run a cost-centre before. Markets also like predictability. Investors like your accuracy. The whole industry of 'fixed mortgages' is based on the beauty and comfort of predictability. To surprise often needs guts.

I hear all that. Yet, I will repeat myself. Surprise the market, surprise your boss, surprise yourself, surprise your followers, surprise your teams, surprise the guys in corporate. I am confident that you know what I mean.

The trade-off is between predictability/safe journey and surprise/leadership. Nobody can argue against safe journeys, so you will be forgiven for 'meeting expectations'. I personally dislike the expression 'exceeding expectations'. It sounds like heavy rain. I prefer surprise, regardless of expectations.

# [80]

# MAKE YOUR TRADE-OFFS TRANSPARENT

In my experience, people can understand budget cuts, but there are several types of acceptance, leading to several levels of embracing and implementing.

Type one: cut across the board, indiscriminately. We need to find savings of x %. This is as frequent as it is silly. There is hardly ever a strategic reason to indiscriminately cut a fixed percentage across the board.

Type two: the savings are required. Don't cut in an indiscriminate way. Make decisions. As long as we can deliver the target, discrimination based on logic is fine. This type gives empowerment to the budget holder and relies on the judgment of the group or division.

Type three: the budget has been reduced, targets have been allocated and we expect you to meet them. Some elements will need divestment, but in other cases you may even consider to invest more. This is unusual, but strictly speaking correct in analytic-decision terms. Investing more in A may indeed give you savings by avoiding having to do B. Decision Analysis professionals see this as normal, but the average manager and finance controller don't agree upfront with this kind of thinking; i.e. investing as a means of cost-cutting.

Type four: we are not doing X (or we are cutting X) because we need to do more of Y. This type is compatible with the others listed above. Its power is in the transparency of the trade-off. Many managers would accept a cut if they knew that the money was not being 'stolen' from them and going to some sort of corporate vaults, but that there is a reason to divert it to somewhere else. They may not like it, but the simple explanation of a transparent trade-off makes the affair acceptable.

For everything we do, there is always something we don't do. It should be simple to express it like this, but for some reason we still prefer a blank 'don't' and we still expect full understanding and commitment.

Trade-off transparency has zero cost and very high impact.

# DOGMATISM BREEDS STRONGER DOGMA

STRATEGY

Paul Krugman, winner of the Nobel Prize for Economics, has made the observation in his column in the New York Times that economic doctrines that prove to be wrong, sometimes tend to lead not to a 'concession of being wrong', but to an even more extreme position in their proponents. He uses the case of inflation-phobia. In 2009, the American Federal Reserve took action to deal with the financial crisis and many politicians and economists predicted that inflation would soar as a consequence. When it did not happen, instead of acknowledging it and 'moving on', many of those prophets said that high inflation was in fact happening, but that the government was concealing it. A great conspiracy theory amongst many.

He draws a parallel with climate change, which for many in the US Republican Party has become, says Krugman, an extreme position, despite all the evidence in favour of global warming. In fact, he says that professing that global warming is a hoax, and subscribing to a global conspiracy theory amongst scientists and politicians, is now almost mandatory for the party.

Perhaps in different ways, we, in organizations present some parallels as well. Despite the overwhelming data showing the phenomenal failures of big Mergers and Acquisitions (M&A) we keep pursuing them as a 'solution', often to desperate situations. History has plenty of examples of M&A catastrophes: Kmart and Sears, eBay and Skype, AOL and Time Warner, Daimler-Benz and Chrysler, HP and Compaq, just to quote some of significant publicity. For each of these 'big public fiascos', there are hundreds of less visible ones where 'integration' failed to deliver. 'Culture' (differences, incompatibilities, etc.) is reason number one.

We also have the case of organizations where rational strategies of effectiveness share a very fine line with dogmatic views on 'what is right'. For example, centralization of shared services, regionalization, consolidation of functions,

203

downsizing to the bare minimum, dismantling of structures in the name of cost efficiency and so on. For every good move in a legitimate direction, there will be a dogma waiting to take over. In some instances, 'economies of scale' have delivered 'fiascos of great scale'. As in Krugman's examples, once some of these strategies have proven meaningless, we see more, as opposed to less of them. Interestingly, some of those companies, and some of those leadership teams, will profess to being 'a learning organization'. Peculiar use of language, that is.

# THE HEALING SMELL OF A CORPORATE BONFIRE.
## (THE HERNÁN CORTÈS EXIT STRATEGY).

The British retailer Marks and Spencer (M&S) has 'Plan A' as the title for their vast corporate and social responsibility programme in the areas of 'sourcing, reducing waste and helping communities'. I still remember years ago when I first asked one of their Directors, why they called it 'Plan A'. It was the perfect question, because it had a permanently ready answer, usually provided with a very happy face and some pride: "*We call it Plan A, simply because there is no Plan B.*" I thought that was brilliant and I still think so. In fact, I didn't know at the time that 'because there is no Plan B' is always the tagline associated to 'Plan A', so I thought that reply was quite cheeky.

If M&S does not have a Plan B for its corporate responsibility, it is because the company is fully committed to its Plan A. Plan A, as an expression of commitment, is the modern version of 'burning your ships' or 'burning your bridges'.

Hernán Cortés conquered Mexico in 1519 with approx. 600 people. He burnt his 11 boats by the beach. He got rid of his plan B. His exit strategy was 'There is no exit'. Alexander the Great did the same in the 4th Century when he invaded Persia.

A few bonfires here and there may be needed in the organization. The bonfire may be made of products, or services, or old strategies. A bit of a burning smell may be very healthy. Whilst we may not be Cortés or Alexander, and not brave enough to burn all the strategic ships at once, the 'No-Exit-no-Plan-B' strategy may in some cases be exactly what is needed to focus people's attention, to mobilize commitment, to re-direct energy or perhaps to conquer a new territory.

The trouble with many corporate and organizational pledges, not just in the area of corporate responsibility, but also in day-to-day leadership, strategy and execution, is that they lack credibility. Perhaps they are simply just not credible in their own right. Perhaps they are potentially credible, but people don't believe the promises.

There is nothing better to focus minds and show commitment than the smell of a good corporate bonfire.

# CUSTOMER
## CUSTOMER-CENTRISM POLICY, MISSING MY EUROSTAR

# I MISSED MY EUROSTAR TRAIN. HOW WONDERFUL! (ME, AS A CASE STUDY)

Last week I was in a hotel and conference centre in Belgium, halfway between Brussels and Antwerp, working with a client on the Kick-Off meeting for a Viral Change™ project. I had arrived late the previous evening, not many people had been around. The man at the bar simply handed me my room key. That was easy, I thought!

The next day I needed to do some printing for my meeting. *"No problem, email it to me at reception."* A few minutes later, the copies were ready. The meeting room was cold. *"No problem."* Minutes later it was fixed and the engineer came to see me personally to make sure it was OK. All in perfect English with a nice Flemish accent.

The meeting went very well. At the end I needed a taxi to go to Brussels Midi train station to get the Eurostar back to the UK. About a 45-minute ride. Small detail: not only was it Friday night; it was also the start of school holidays. The traffic was static for miles in and around Brussels. No taxis to be had.

209

What do you mean? The man at reception spent half an hour non-stop looking for taxis from five different companies. That is all he does.

In the meantime, I asked for the manager. When she came to see me I said how impressed I was and told her about the good service they had provided. She said they were going to have a short party that evening to celebrate the (late!) New Year and that she was going to share this with her people. But five minutes later the lady from the cafeteria waved at me from a distance with a perfectible audible, *"Thanks for the compliment!"*

Finally, a taxi arrives. The taxi driver convinced me that driving to Brussels would be foolish. He offered to take me to the train station at the airport instead of taking me to the Brussels Eurostar station (at the other side of Brussels). From there, I could take a quick train into the city. OK! Since I was going to the airport I wanted to check with my office to see if there were any flights. My UK office, adamant that they had checked (all flights full) would try again. Before I could articulate anything on the phone, the taxi driver used an app on his phone (traffic was slow!) and said, *"You may want to check BA 339 at 18.15. Do you want me to call them?"* Wow!

Long story short: no flights available. We arrived at the car park at the airport near the train station - which is not the same as 'the train station'. The taxi driver insisted on parking and taking my luggage to the ticket office, as it was not obvious to me where that would be. He waited until I got to the right entrance for the right track of the right train. He had paid for the car park. I insisted on paying for that, he refused, but I managed to slip 10 Euros into his pocket. That train took me to the centre of Brussels, what a relief! Then, for some strange late Friday evening dysfunctional reason, I get off one stop too soon. Wrong move! Another taxi.

# CUSTOMER

So after all that, I reach the Eurostar station late for my train. I just missed it! My ticket was non-changeable, non-refundable (a recurrent false economy habit) so I asked for a new one. The lady at the counter said with a big smile: "*Just this time, enjoy dinner*" and she swaps the old non-changeable, non-refundable ticket for a new non-changeable, non-refundable one... on the next train!

What happened next after this little epidemic of kindness is as follows: I said thanks to the lady serving my meal (a disproportionate number of times), I carried and moved the luggage of an elderly lady (beyond my normal courtesy), I lent a couple of pounds to a coffee-desperate American girl in the train bar, and I wished the train manager a good weekend (he replied 'muchas gracias' – perhaps he had noticed my accent).

Although not a fan of case studies, this was without knowing it a live case study for my book *Homo Imitans*. The little epidemic of kind acts had triggered a second little epidemic in me. People copy each other. It's not rational! We are very sophisticated copying machines. I used to say to clients, if you have an epidemic of nastiness, you want a counter-epidemic of kindness, not a training programme for the nasty people. It was all in my book and then here it was in my life. Behaviours are copied, not trained. Missing the Eurostar was the least of my problems.

# TO CREATE A CULTURE OF CUSTOMER FOCUS: USE ONE!

Disclaimer: I don't have any shares in the company, nor do I receive any discounts or commissions!

No place I know can match the Châteauform houses as venues for meetings. But you need to live in (or travel to) France to enjoy most of them. There are only a few of them in other European countries.

Châteauform is an all-inclusive hotel and meeting venue chain dedicated to business. Every single aspect of the use is included in the price, from your impeccable bedroom to the projectors in the meeting room. In fact, Châteauform venues are 'houses' (big ones!) managed by a family (and plenty of staff) who greet you personally at reception. Well, there is no reception as such, because it's a 'house', you are free to roam and serve yourself and generally make yourself at home. (A client of mine said, "*I wish this were my house...*")

Espresso machines everywhere, the bar well-stocked (no service. Remember, it's your house, grab the gin yourself) and every single detail is worked out. You need water for your bedroom? OK, there are baskets with bottles in every corner, corridor or stairs, or perhaps in a basket in front of your room. It's very sunny outside, perhaps too sunny? Well, there are baskets at the door full of sunglasses of all colours and shapes – serve yourself- and those other baskets with hats of all sizes - pick one that suits you and go out, enjoy yourself. For winter, there will be piles of blankets in front of the patio doors. In the business meeting areas – where every service is included, from sound system to projection, to flipcharts to electronic boards – there will be a photocopy machine. No, no code. Dozens of wireless handsets around 'the house' will allow you to call anybody to come and help you if needed, on anything, at any time.

Your breaks area may have a constant supply of drinks and food, not at fixed times 'on your agenda'. At lunchtime there is a starter buffet, but then you go to the kitchen and talk to the chefs personally about your desired dishes. Serve yourself with the wine you choose, they are all lined up.

Anything you need, from an umbrella to games in the gardens, to extra notepads, is there available to you, included in the price. The Châteauform at which I recently stayed also had a gym. In true Châteauform spirit you would find a selection of trainers at the door. Of course! There was also a collection of green rubber garden boots, all possible sizes, in front of the garden doors.

Founded by people from Club Méditerranée – Club Med, for those who know this firm– they have managed to re-create the same 'all-inclusive-it-is-your-house' atmosphere for business. Attention to the customer and personalized treatment is simply exquisite. Once, when I was too late, I was brought breakfast at the meeting room by somebody from the kitchen in a golf cart, and I found my international newspaper outside the same meeting room during a break. All this is done with zero levels of silly servility. It's just...normal.

So I have two questions. One, why on earth has this not been copied by a million other business venues, where we have to suffer a de-personalized and robotic treatment and extra charges for some third grade biscuits and bad coffee? Two, why is 'customer service' the easiest thing to do, something that does not need to be (re)invented, but also the most difficult thing to find?

Customer focus is, in many places, all lip service and of no substance. We all know that. If you want to study a culture of customer-centrism, or have a meeting about customer focus, go to a Châteauform venue. Even if you have to fly there.

# CUSTOMER-CENTRIC? PROVE IT!

Many organizations want to be customer-centric and will do lots of things to at least move in that direction. The standard translation of this desire looks like a series of statements or aspirations. For example, there will be a code or a value system saying: *"Understand the customer, listen to customers, empathize with the customer, be customer-centric, etc."*

For those of us on the behavioural side of the spectrum, these things that people are expected to do or to be, do not meet any behavioural standards. So, it is impossible to do anything with them when shaping a culture. Why? Behaviours create cultures! The terms listed above don't have unequivocal meaning, which is one of the key characteristics of a behaviour. So, these things are not behaviours.

I don't really know what 'understand', 'listen', 'empathize' or 'be' mean. Well, I do. But I am not sure they mean the same to everyone or that you and I are speaking the same language. Whilst I can say I am listening, you may say that I am not, that you don't agree that I am, etc. I may empathize, as far as I am concerned, but you may think I'm not. You may have a very different concept of empathy. Who is right? That is the wrong question. Nobody is wrong. But these concepts are equivocal. They are bad currency in cultural terms.

In behavioural terms, 'the proof is in the pudding'. Imagine that everybody in the management team or group must bring a fresh customer insight to the table every time they meet. To do that, everybody would need to have spoken to at least one customer, which means that they would have listened to them, which would have made these people customer-centric (at least for a bit). So, 'understand', 'listen', 'empathize' or 'be...', which are equivocal in meaning, will now have been translated into something very concrete, very visible and behavioural: 'always bring a fresh customer insight' (to the table, to the discussion, to the conversation, to the review). This is the behaviour. The rest is a set of aspirations, expected language, but not very useful for a behaviour-driven building of culture, as we do in Viral Change™.

My validity test is this: Imagine 100 people this afternoon starting their meetings with "*Here is my fresh customer insight*". The organization will be customer-centric without a single session of training in customer-centrism.

Imagine that...

# 'IT'S OUR POLICY'
# IS OFTEN THE WORST POLICY

A while ago, my brand new iPhone was stolen at the airport, when I had left it behind on a table for just a few minutes. Clever thief, stupid me! I had just acquired the phone with a data package from my carrier. I called my carrier. Since I had a business account, I expected that a handset replacement would be easy to obtain. I did not expect it to be free. I was prepared to pay whatever was required. When I called them and explained the circumstances, they told me repeatedly that 'it was not their policy' to replace a phone, even if I paid. The phone came with a package and that was that. One contract, one phone. No provision to have a second one, even if I paid.

His level of sympathy was zero. The 'It's not our policy to do that' was repeated several times by the 'customer services representative' at the beginning of each of his sentences, no matter what. When I challenged him that I needed help, not a lecture on their policies, he suggested that I try their competitor! Literally. Because 'it was their policy not to replace a handset', of course! Today, I am with another carrier.

But I didn't go to their competitor at the time, because I

decided to call Apple directly. A human being with a Californian accent (I was in the UK) was at the other end in less than a minute (compared with the close to five minutes it took to get through to my service provider). I explained the incident from the airport and how bad (stupid?) I felt. The voice at the other end started a conversation about how dreadful it was to have your phone stolen, how bad one feels and how having a hard time with this is the last thing one wants on a busy day. And he went as far as saying, "*I feel sorry for you.*" I could not believe it. There was a human being at the other end of the line with empathy for my little troubles and he was truly sympathetic and kind. Had he tried to sell me a fridge, I would have bought it. But I bought a new iPhone from him. Before he went off, we chatted about the weather in California and the UK.

In the last few weeks, I have tried to book a hotel for a family weekend trip to Ireland. The hotel reservation person told me that, for that particular weekend, they had a policy of not accepting a booking for less than 2 nights. I only needed one. I expressed my surprise. I confess I had not encountered this before. "*Sorry Sir, it is our policy that during these busy weekends, we don't book for less than 2 nights.*" I protested and she suggested that I write to the manager. So I did. Guess what the manager's email said? That 'it's our policy', etc. I did email the general manager to test if he hired his staff from Robots Anonymous. His reply came with a familiar statement: 'It's our policy that', etc.

These examples of self-centred-not-customer-services are not uncommon. People who are supposed to serve you don't listen to you and show zero interest in actually serving you. None of these people at that hotel spontaneously suggested any alternatives to me. But I know a bit more about policies now. And I still think an Apple fridge is a good idea.

# THERE IS ONLY ONE 'CUSTOMER' AND HE PAYS THE BILLS

I am your customer, you are my customer. When I need to provide you with something, you are my customer. When you need to do the same for me, I am your customer. I am marketing, you, the finance department, are my customer when you ask me for data. I am corporate finance, you, country finance, are my customers. I am R&D, my customer is marketing and sales. I am sales, my customers are the consumers. I am information management, the rest of the company is my customer.

The customer-centric mantra that has been in place for many years has created this muddle. Not pronouncing the word 'customer' has become so politically incorrect that we tend to flood our thinking and our language with it, to make sure we don't miss it.

There is a historical point and reason behind this. Many organizations work in silo mode with low-grade cross-communication and cross-collaboration, so it made sense at some point to inject a bit of 'consumer mentality' to make the point that we are all serving each other, in one way or another, within the organization.

However, by over customer-izing the language, the real customer gets lost or neglected. There is only one real customer: the one who pays the bill. This is the external customer: an individual in the case of the Business to Customer (B2C) scenario and a company in the Business-to-Business (B2B) scenario. Anything else is just muddled thinking.

I encourage my clients to make language choices. The internal 'I serve you, you serve me' may need a different language: call it client, business partner, co-worker, co-dependent, chum, internal service provider... I am playing silly language games here on purpose. But find a term, other than 'customer,' so that we can have a real conversation about the real customer. So a simple rule such as 'the customer is always external' could do

# CUSTOMER

the trick. Of course, there may be more than one external customer.

Cleaning up internal language is important.

Customer-izing the internal organization may be nice and rewarding. It may create a good feeling of cooperation, but it often dilutes the external focus. And since many companies spend 90% of their time looking inwards and 10% outwards, a bit of 'externalization of the customer language' would do just nicely.

# [88]

# YOU MUST UNDERSTAND, WE ARE A BIG COMPANY

I was told this story a long time ago. A CEO of a large company gets a letter from a well-known, big, market-leading removals company.

*"Dear Mr CEO, we are aware of the impending move of your headquarters from Manchester to London and we would like to offer you our first-class, award-winning customer-focused, all-in-one, comprehensive removal services."* The CEO replied back: *"Dear X, thanks very much for your kind offer, which we appreciate greatly. I have, however, three concerns. Number one: the move is not from Manchester to London, but from London to Manchester. Number two: it's not impending, we have already moved. Number three: your company moved us!"*

The well-known, big, market-leading removals company wrote back: *"I am sorry for the misunderstanding. You will appreciate that we are a big company and I did not know that."*

To screw up on three fronts is bad enough, but asking to be understood on the grounds of 'we are a big company' is downright arrogance, big time. What it implies is that: *"we are a big company and therefore we don't know what is going on, and we should be allowed to not know what is going on. Forgive us; it's all down to how big/important/busy/we are."* The fact that the writer of the letter did not seem to be embarrassed, says it all.

How many times do we associate 'big' with 'power' and in turn attribute special permissions for minor peccadilloes such as getting customer insights wrong! Amazon is a very big company, it welcomes me by my name all the time, it knows exactly who I am, what I've bought, what I am likely to buy and what they need to recommend to me. Amazon knows me. Well, their algorithms do.

Big, small, medium-sized, developed market, developing market, American, French, Italian, British, product company, service company: any one of these can be good or bad. Good management does not depend on size or culture. 'Forgive me, we are a big company' no longer gets you any sympathy or credit. In fact, it may even be a reason to avoid using your services.

# ORGANIZING OURSELVES

## STAYING IN BETA, REBOOT,

# SELF-MANAGEMENT,

## ELEPHANTS,
## THE VICTORIANS

# THE COMPANY ON A TREADMILL: THE BENEFITS OF ROUTINE STRESS TESTS

Banks have had stress tests imposed to see how they would cope with difficult market conditions. For example, in the US, a typical stress scenario in the past has been: 50 per cent drop in equity prices; 21 per cent decline in housing prices; unemployment at 13 per cent. Regulators will then use that to 'see' how a particular bank would do under these circumstances. They will assess its responses, its reserves, etc. Then they will issue a pass... or not.

Hardware and software products have stress tests to see how they will react under given circumstances. People undergo cardiac stress tests to see what would happen with your heart during extra-ordinary effort. Doctors put people on treadmills and examine an electrocardiogram during forced, non-normal circumstances. It helps to uncover possible hidden anomalies.

Organizations should also have stress tests. I am not talking about tests for their financial conditions, but for the organizational system. Some examples of real life 'stress situations' are:

- An acquisition that, although always a possibility, had not been expected so soon. It will divert lots of attention and resources and will create great disruption.
- New products that are launched too close after one another, but that can't be changed. There will be a 6-month mad peak followed by prolonged calm.
- Recruitment is much slower than predicted and there will be significant and prolonged resource gaps beyond expectations.
- The sudden departure or illness of a member of the top leadership team in charge of a delicate business area will require a caretaker, extending the already unstable situation.

Other sources of stress tests may be a technological crisis, product recalls or a complicated or hostile merger, for example.

Management teams should simulate these scenarios and map possible reactions. It is the equivalent of military manoeuvres. It's not difficult and has zero cost. The first step is to define which situations will put the company under sudden stress, list them and agree on a few top ones to examine. Agree on the criteria to pass the test. Then simulate responses and imagine bad and less-bad scenarios. List reactions and assess the cost (not just monetary). Have you passed?

One of our expectations of leaders is that they will have this great ability to project and imagine the future. But, we are not very good at this in organizations. Despite a myriad of SWOT analysis and scenario planning techniques, people usually revert to a linear, predictable, extrapolated world in the crafting of a Business or Strategic Plan.

228

# ORGANIZING OURSELVES

If I could have 100 pounds (or dollars) for every Scenario Planning flipchart sheet that was stuck on a wall after many exhausting hours, only to be ignored by moving on to the next item on the agenda (e.g. the business plan itself), I could have a few exotic holidays or a trip around the world.

Stress tests should be routine in any planning process. It's the company on a treadmill. It's called a health check.

And they should be marked on your calendar.

# 'THE DUNBAR NUMBER' AND 'MAD LEAN NUMBERS': A QUESTION OF THE RIGHT CRITICAL MASS OF PEOPLE TO MAKE THINGS HAPPEN

# ORGANIZING OURSELVES

Robin Dunbar, an anthropologist, psychologist and professor at Oxford, has formulated that 150 was the "*cognitive limit to the number of individuals with whom any one person can maintain stable social relationships*". Since then, this has been known as 'the Dunbar number'. Its application to Organizational Architecture is obvious. Units of more than 150 people would theoretically struggle to form proper social relationships. Corollary: you'd better break a large set-up into smaller 'Dunbar pieces' if you want to keep proper conversations, meaningful management and a sense of community.

Some people have questioned the threshold of 150 and have done so from different angles, but not many have suggested a number above 200. Whether it is 150 plus or minus fifty, the principle stands. At some point on the scale-up of the organization (growth, M&A, consolidation) there is a threshold beyond which the total number of people will work against the community, fluid communication, ethos and style that, in theory, many small organizations and start-ups have. In other words, the often invoked and desired 'need to keep an entrepreneurial spirit' is very much dependent on the structure of the organization, its networks and the size of its component pieces.

Interestingly, not many people have looked at the opposite end of the spectrum. If above 150 you face certain risks, below some 'minimal critical mass' you will suffer from a completely different set of risks. The lean structures preached in the last decades sometimes mean zero slack in the system. With zero slack, knowledge sharing is impossible, company memory is deleted every time somebody leaves and work and efficiency become a struggle. 'Cutting to the bone' in structural terms is simply madness. I call them 'Mad Lean numbers'. One single individual doing a critical job, with zero knowledge transfer, is Mad Lean. No sensible organization should have Units of One as working units, without shadowing, each of them at high risk (leaving, being ill) and with high replacement costs. This is not efficient management, it's simply bad management or, indeed, mad management.

We are so afraid of overlapping or shadowing jobs that it has become politically incorrect to suggest them. Western management calls this a waste, redundancy or inefficiency. It's not. Both the Dunbar Number on the scale-up side and my Mad Lean numbers on the minimalist side are key components of managerial maths. They can't be ignored.

# FROM THE MOVIE-MAKING SCHOOL OF MANAGEMENT

Let's make a movie. We need a producer with the money. A director to direct. An agency to find the actors. Lighting people? Yes, please. Outdoors or indoors? We need the guys in charge of location. Ah, we need studios as well. And the special effects crew. Don't forget the editors. I am sure I am still missing a few tribes.

Who is really, really in charge? Surely the producer? Well, not really, he has the money and certainly a lot of influence, but he is not directing. What about the lighting and casting and location guys? Well, they're not in charge, but nobody can do anything without them, so they are sort of in charge. Ah, the Special Effects people! It's a movie with lots of effects, so they are in charge. Not really, they only care about big screens and keyboards. And anyway, they're all under 25.

Ok then, let's ask a typical organizational question. Who reports to whom? *"Sorry, I don't understand reporting, please explain"*, the movie people would say. But, how does it work? Who calls the shots? *"Well, it depends on the type of shots, the days we are shooting and a few other things."*

It sounds like chaos! *"Chaos? It's been working this way for many decades now."* At this point of the discussion, somebody is bound to say: *"Wait a minute, the movie is the movie; finally, there will be a movie on the screen and it will have a big name associated with it, that's the director. It's the director's baby, so surely he's in charge?"*

Nope. The movie you see on the screen is not the director's movie. The editor has made the cuts and delivers the final movie, which excludes many things the director filmed. And, yes, the director can get very annoyed. That is why there are versions called 'The Director's Cut', in other words, the unadulterated version. But go and try to find one of these.

So here we are: several tribes just get together for a while. They all know what to do, nobody is really in charge, they do their jobs and show up when needed, they disappear when finished and everybody gets paid. No committees, no task forces, no employee engagement surveys. Group, ungroup, have fun and no org chart!

Before you think of the 27 reasons why 'this will never work' in your organization, I suggest we pause. Maybe we are missing something here by looking at things solely from the perspective of the 'traditional' organization. Maybe we should all try to think about the making of an organizational movie.

Cut!

THE
SELF-
MANAGEMENT
TRAIN HAS LEFT THE
STATION.
**THE JOURNEY** IS VERY
BUMPY.
ARRIVAL TIME TBD.
WATCH OUT FOR
UPDATES

The historical existence of several layers of management in any organization may be related to its size. In a command-and-control firm of some size, managers ensure that objectives are declared and then check in with people who are doing the work to see what's going on. They absorb the information of the feedback loop and pass it on upwards. They assess the efficacy and effectiveness of the tasks and assign a reward. Forgive me, I know it's a caricature of the 'managerial picture'.

As channels of communication within the firm became multi-centric (not just top-down and back up again), communication was digitalized and the inter-dependence of groups within the company became almost impossible to represent on an organization chart. 'Management' as a function and as a box on the organization chart started to look redundant. Today, much more than just a few years ago, it is possible to have groups of individuals in the organization teaming up, perfectly capable of doing their jobs, without any direct command and control. Effectively they could be/are self-managed and populated by self-assigned people. Middle management is starting to look superfluous, amongst other things, because it's less and less clear what 'middle' means, other than perhaps an 'information traffic control hub' (with the manager simply being an 'information traffic warden').

The self-management train has left the station, but it's not short of challenges for the journey ahead. For starters, we don't have good maps and toolkits. All management, organization and leadership development and other 'HR' navigation tools were created at a time when the business environment was more linear, the world outside the firm much more predictable and the division of labour within the firm in need of a strict and efficient top-down, command-and-control information system.

Behind these old toolkits were Academia and the Big Consulting Firms, pretty much the same people who now preach a rethinking, a revolution or even the death of management. They have a great track record in teaching how to manage an organization, but hardly any on how to deal with an organism. The modern firm is a social organism. We have very few good toolkits for this and even the good ones won't pass the paternity test of Academia or Big Consulting. Management education continues to de-educate with old toolkits.

One of the main problems of the self-management train is that, in many cases, self-management is imposed on the firm as a fashion, mantra or copy of another firm where it seems to work. Get ready for some shocked faces when companies try to be the next version of Zappos. However, the direction is inexorably set and I strongly recommend at least some level of experimentation in your organization. The sky will not fall. The potential is enormous.

Although people are hearing the self-management music, many of those same people can become very confused. For example, 'self-management' has zero to do with 'leader-less' organizations. Any social (animal) grouping will have leaders. If they are not formally installed, they will emerge. Self-management simply requires different leadership.

One year ago, my team and I started the formal work that we call 'Building Remarkable Organizations'. One of the ten 'Lego pieces' we use is the self-management progression.

Let me share my number one rule: since self-management is a 'when' question, not an 'if' question, 'eyes closed' or 'head in the sand' are not good strategies. It's time to understand the itinerary of that train so that one can figure out at which stations it may be possible to hop on. It does not have to be the next one.

# STAY IN 'BETA'

# ORGANIZING OURSELVES

The traditional organization is, amongst other things, obsessed with closure. It despises ambiguity and puts a premium on the absolute clarity of processes, systems and structures. It's engineered to run on testosterone. Inputs produce outputs and they'd better be good since all those inputs are so expensive!

It's a military operation even when we say it isn't. But even the military have discovered that the world around us is volatile, unpredictable, complex and ambiguous. They have even an acronym for it: VUCA. And if you are in this VUCA world, you can't afford high levels of 'uncertainty-avoidance' (a classical cultural hallmark of many traditional organizations). That world is uncertainty in itself; so, to avoid uncertainty is to avoid the world completely. I often think that the military have become much better at navigating ambiguity than we are in organizations.

The enemy is VUCA, not a specific country anymore! Can you believe it?

In this world of moving targets (markets, competitors, technology, pace of creation/destruction, predictability of anything, Black Swans...), to have everything crafted, well-structured, closed, finished, stable and strong is suicidal. People with all the answers should be disqualified from holding leadership office. This is not in praise of chaos, but more a call for a well-organized, un-finished, un-settled, un-stable, not completely closed, imperfect organization with enough room to manoeuvre and adapt at the speed of light. I call this 'Unfinished by Design' or the 'Beta Organization'.

If you want to succeed, stay in beta. Lots of alpha organizations are either dead or are not feeling very well.

# [94]

# FOR EVERY PROBLEM, THE VICTORIANS HAD A BUILDING

About seven years ago, the BBC broadcasted a series called *How we built Britain*, presented by David Dimbleby. In the episode dedicated to the Victorians, he said something, almost in passing, which has stuck in my mind ever since: *"For every problem, the Victorians had a building."*

Growing local government? OK, here we are: big City Halls (Manchester, Leeds...). Mental illness? Sure, the big asylums were built in the form of 'mini-towns' (all services included), which the great Canadian sociologist, Erving Goffman (1922-1982), would call 'Total Institutions'. Mass transportation? No problem, railways and their cathedral-like train stations appeared. Big churches, big shopping malls (probably not called this) and big leisure centres also sprung to life. 'The building' was the answer. And the bigger, the better.

'Management' is the 'Victorian Architecture' of the modern organization. For every problem we create a structure: a new business unit, a new franchise, a new committee, a new task

240

force, a new merger of A and B, a new management team, a restructuring, a new structural or functional conceptual building as 'the answer'. We have become very good at providing structural solutions even to problems that may, for example, require behavioural answers. A typical scenario is amalgamating A and B into C because A and B do not talk to each other. We create a new structure C, but people are still not talking to each other. (Mind you, we did save a Senior VP salary.)

The Big Guys of the consulting industry have sold us '(re)structure' as the answer to everything. In part, because permutations of the Organization Chart are an easy thing to do. If you want to be seen doing something, change the structure.

Small detail, 'the building' may not be the answer'. In fact, 'the new building' may be a big distraction and create an illusion of 'problem solved'.

I am bound to say this because of my background and my own work, but for every managerial problem we should first look for a behavioural answer. It's a better bet.

# WE BUY AN ELEPHANT AND THEN WE TRAIN THE ELEPHANT TO BEHAVE LIKE A GAZELLE

What would be wrong with buying gazelles in the first place? The answer I sometimes hear is, "*Well, the market has plenty of elephants. Plus, elephants are strong, have experience, particularly the ones who belong to big herds of... elephants. Besides, we have always bought elephants; we know elephants, we have a whole Department of Procurement dedicated to Elephants.*"

We hire people with an excellent pedigree in Big Corporate and then we put them in charge of the start-up, with assets that include six months funding in the bank, three guys and a telephone...

We create a new division with lots of VPs, lots of functions, lots of titles and we ask them to 'think differently'...

We fill all the recruitment gaps in the five management teams of the five affiliates, following the same patterns and profile, and then we get them together in a big off-site meeting to talk about 'culture change'...

We hire ambitious, high adrenaline, no-prisoners-taken, over-achieving, individualistic, Darwinian sales people and then we ask them to work as a team...

There are always natural windows of opportunity in the decision making of the organization beyond which any reversal will have a significant cost. And the monetary cost is not always the most significant one. Training elephants to become gazelles (or gazelles to become elephants) does not sound like a good idea. But this is what we are doing all the time. If you have an open window in front of you (the chance to completely re-think whether you need elephants, gazelles or no animals at all), make sure you don't close it!

Incidentally, I am not suggesting that ex-Big-Corporate people cannot run start-ups. I am suggesting that it takes a particular ex-Big-Corporate mind to do it and that they often underestimate the challenges of working in an almost zero-support environment. I am also saying that you can't have it both ways: love entrepreneurship and hire Big Corporate expertise; love diversity and hire clones; love collaboration and teamwork and choose individual contributions.

# THE COMPANY WILL REBOOT ITSELF FROM FRIDAY TO SATURDAY. APOLOGIES. SERVICES WILL BE LIMITED DURING THIS PERIOD.

I like the concept of reinvention, renewal or transformation. But most of all, I like the concept of rebooting! Organizations, teams, groups and even entire companies always reach a plateau at some point. The point in the curve where things are OK, but not brilliant; there is nothing wrong, but also nothing exceptional or remarkable; no particular problems, but not many new ideas. Things are stable, there is no crisis, people turnover is low and all is fine, thank you. "*You have reached the un-remarkable destination*", your organizational 'Sat Nav' seems to say. It's time to reboot the system.

One of the programmes I have designed under the banner of our 'Accelerators' is called 'Reboot!' We ask people to find the elephants in the room, the sacred cows, the things that need urgent health checks. We then make an inventory of mistakes and successes, etc. What one can do in one single day of Reboot! is simply amazing. A Game Plan is then easy to create.

Regardless of how you do it or what you call it, you need to plan, not only for 'essential maintenance', as many digital services and their websites do from time to time, but for a full reboot! Look inside, up and down, sideways, dust here and there, question the unquestionable, open the windows, allow fresh air in, imagine, inject some disruption, reboot!

This healthy shakeup can be planned. Actually, it is a hundred times better when scheduled, as opposed to when you are forced to do it in a crisis or under stress. Schedule some 'reboot time' in the life cycle of your organization, no matter what; even if you are at, what you consider, the peak of your performance. Stop, push the button, have the courage to pause, listen, then re-start.

The old lithium batteries that we used to have in older devices and phones came with the warning to discharge them completely from time to time and then charge again, otherwise the continuous use and daily charge would make charging less and less effective. Eventually, the battery life will be minimal. Well, organizations today are still in lithium battery mode. Follow the advice. Schedule rebooting. Abandon the plateau, even if it is a comfortable one. You can reach greater heights!

# THE UN-REACHABLE WORK FORCE: WHAT NGOS WITH REMOTE OPERATIONS TEACH US ABOUT ORGANIZING WORK

Many years ago, I learnt from the UNHCR, the UN refugee Agency, that many global NGOs of that kind had invented the art of employee engagement at a distance.

We were discussing organizational modes within companies and a Director of UNHCR was with us. The conversation evolved towards decentralized operations, the pros and cons of 'control', and the challenges of managing a workforce that's remote and that you don't see. The director looked at us with an incredulous look and said: "*This is what we do all the time.*" So the formula was (and I'm paraphrasing): clear directions, lots of trust, get reports when you can, send feedback.

That organization and similar ones did not have the time or opportunity to ponder levels of control (on the ground): control was near zero in some instances.

It has always fascinated me how there would be constant learning, if only business was smart enough to look for models outside their mental frameworks. I have written before about 'the movie model', one of many examples we could benefit from digging into.

Large, field-based NGOs are also a good start. Not just for organizational models per se, but also for learnings about leadership, employee engagement and decision making.

# THE BATTLE FOR THE 3S'S:
# SYNTHESIS, SENSE AND SIMPLICITY

Let me share with you my 3S's, where I suggest you put your money:

**1. Synthesis**: My followers, readers and clients know that I keep coming back to this. We have populated our organizations with Super Analytical Tribes that are able to dissect an elephant into pieces and create beautiful PhDs, Strategic Plans and Competitor Analyses of legs, trunks, tusks, ears, etc. We've competed on skills based on these specialized abilities: *"My trunk experts are the best in the industry"*, *"this is a place that attracts the top tusk specialists"*, etc. However, we need people who are able to recognize an elephant when they see an elephant. Perhaps shout: *"Psst! It's an elephant!"* Then we also need people who can re-construct the elephant once the Dissectors (not Directors) have done their jobs.

**2. Sense**: Inundated with information, data, options and the complexity of business life, organizations and their leaders have progressive difficulty in distinguishing between noise and signal. Sometimes everything looks like a priority. Everything seems to make sense (but it doesn't). Choices are difficult to make. Our 'prioritizing' tools are primitive. Huge brainstorming sessions are often followed by a reductionist approach that ends up focusing on doing what is doable, under our control and looks like providing immediate benefit: quick wins. However, what may make real sense is to focus on what seems to be less doable, the things we can't fully control and for which the benefits have yet to be defined. The key lies in what has been left out. Making sense of it all, above and beyond the apparent pseudo-logic of the priority-setting exercise, is a skill in short supply. Sense making, sound judgement, identifying the signal: please bring them all. Don't stop the prioritization and brainstorming, but remember the brain attached to the storm and make good use of it.

**3. Simplicity**: Simplicity does not mean reducing something complex to digestible bits (the elephant parts above), but it means de-cluttering processes, systems and procedures. It's about being mindful of the overgrown garden that nobody seems to tidy up; the overgrown grass and shrubs that everybody seems to be happy about. Simplicity can coexist with complex business provided that the complexity has been de-cluttered and the unnecessary removed. In our corporate world, simplicity is often understood as reductionism: the bullet points, the executive summary, the elevator pitch. These things make us feel good, but may not solve complexity. Indeed, we may be fooled by the 'reduced amount of information' and by the pristine, reduced 'summary'.

Most of these 3S's can be found somewhere in my previous books, particularly in *New Leaders Wanted, Now Hiring*! The topics come back to me again and again.

The 3S's are still largely unresolved although we kid ourselves that we have sorted it all out through elephant cutting, post-it prioritizing, executive summaries.

Yeah, sure!

# [99]

# THE BEST OF A PLUS THE BEST OF B MAY BE CRAP

Automatic pilot thinking during a merger says: let's take the best of company A and the best of company B to create the new company C. The catch is that the best of A plus the best of B may not be good enough for C. To put it unkindly, the sum of the two "best" may still be crap! The focus should be: what should the new C look like? By all means, let's take any goodness from anywhere it is available, but you now have an opportunity to build something above and beyond the past. If we don't realize that, we may settle for the 'obvious' (and easier) common denominator and this does not automatically make it good. Ok, it's harder to think this way, I admit. But I would bet my money that in 9 out of 10 cases, the resulting 'C hybrid' (best + best) is not a good idea. Hybrids are bad news. They still contain A-people and B-people and their endless refrain: 'We in A did, we in B run...' Reboot the system. Seize the opportunity to make a brand-new, shiny C.

The best of the past may not be the future you need.

# YOU DON'T HAVE TO ATTEND EVERY ARGUMENT TO WHICH YOU ARE **INVITED**

This quote is from an unknown author. He or she must have known a thing or two about the futility of engaging in every single discussion that comes your way. The quote is also a proxy for 'pick your battles'. There are battles worth fighting and battles that are not. It may also serve as a reflection for leaders on what they choose to do.

In organizational life, people are often pulled in too many directions, where 'signal' and 'noise' get confused all the time. Big things get buried under small things. The important gets confused with the urgent. The strategic and the tactical become mixed up. All things become equally important, equally relevant, equally necessitating a response: to have a say, to send an 'I agree' message...

I am not fond of the word 'prioritization'. Not that I don't believe in the need to prioritize, but I have little faith in our standard ways of doing this. For leaders, a better angle is 'What will make the difference?' Or better, 'What can I personally do, that will make a difference?'

We need to switch from spending our time on 'managing the inevitable' to leading what will not happen unless we lead it. In this quest, you, as a leader, don't have to attend every argument to which you are invited, you don't have to get involved in everything and you certainly do not have to spend your time fighting every battle.

The magic word is choice. There is always a choice: make it!

# YES, I CAN
## (PROFILE YOU).
### LESSONS FROM POLITICAL MARKETING FOR THE
## RUNNING OF ORGANIZATIONS

Political campaigns like the 2008 and 2012 Obama campaigns have clearly understood and mastered the art of profiling. Hardly a new concept, but these campaigns (particularly the one of 2012) have elevated profiling to levels of maximum sophistication. In its simplest translation, a connected mum, very active in the local school and worried about funding for or the quality of education, gets no personal message from the local activists about healthcare reform, youth employment or the trade balance, let alone the terrorist threat. A 90-year old activist campaigning from his bedroom with a laptop (loaded with data) and a phone (there are public videos showing this), is not targeting 20-year olds and talking about unemployment, he is speaking to other people of a similar age and discussing Medicare.

Does it make sense? Yes, it does, of course. But, if it does, we, in business organizations have lost the plot, because we do not segment anybody, other than in performance terms. And talent management is divided into high, medium, average, underperforming, etc. That's it!

The top-down communication systems on which most management practices are based, assume equality and uniformity. Translation: everybody is equal, everybody needs to hear the (same) message and everybody needs to get the same pack of PowerPoints cascaded down throughout the organization. I described this as 'World I' in *Homo Imitans*. Town Hall meetings, top-down communications from management, departmental briefings: they all get the same messages. It's like a one big, single Annual Report downloaded to each brain on the payroll. Companies may be good at external segmentation (customers), but they are very poor at internal segmentation. One message, sent out in tsunami mode.

The Obama campaign's mega-profiling was possible due to the smart use of gigantic amounts of data, sophisticated technology and an obsession with de-centralization and a focus on the grassroots. Incidentally, the Republican Party had access to the

256

same data, but was very bad at using it. The technology failed them and they were not as de-centralized and localized as the Obama camp. You can argue that we, in organizations, are not even close to having the richness of data that political campaigns have about citizens. Sure. But we don't even try to tailor anything within the organization. When it comes to customers, we have segmentation data. When it comes to the workforce, we have names on the payroll, salaries and organization charts. If we accept that the Obama managers 'knew their voters', we should also accept that we, in business organizations, 'don't know our employees'.

# THE THREE MAGIC WORDS: TRANSPARENCY, **CLARITY** AND FAIRNESS

These three organizational 'magic words' get mixed up a lot. It's hard to believe because they are so different. But people love interchanging them. It seems that the use of language in organizational life has a sort of 'complete freedom', which results in lots of 'prêt-a-porter' concepts. So, 'magic' here has to be interpreted as producing an abracadabra effect: use them and many doors will open (even if their meaning is all mixed up).

More than once I have seen these three magic words in a single value system as if their combination validates the good intentions of the company and provides a stamp of integrity and honesty (incidentally, two more words in the magic league).

Organizations seem to thrive on conceptual muddle. My friend, business partner and brilliant inter-cultural consultant, David Trickey, calls this 'a conspiracy of self-inflicted ambiguity'.

My street definitions, to dispel the magic a bit are as follows:

- Transparency: everybody can see it, no secrets.
- Clarity: everybody understands.
- Fairness: nobody is discriminated against.

That's it!

Something may be transparent to the staff, but remain unclear, even opaque to them. Something may be clear for management, but not transparent to others. Something may be fair to people, but not necessarily clear or transparent.

Problems arise when there is a free, interchangeable use of the three. People tend to assume that something is unfair when it's not transparent. But transparency does not automatically make it fair. There is nothing unfair about not making something transparent to everybody. It may or may not be unfair. Some managers preach transparency, but they mean clarity. Other managers preach fairness on the basis of clarity and transparency to all. But the issue may be very unfair, yet clear.

I suggest you carry on playing with the permutations, but avoid at any cost the indiscriminate use. Beware of the prolongation of the 'self-inflicted ambiguity'.

I hope I am clear, that I have been transparent in my intentions and that you find these points fair. If not, I will have to start again.

EVERY
SUCCESSFUL COMPANY'S
GROWTH CONTAINS
SEEDS OF
FAILURE.
AT SOME POINT,
ORGANIZATIONAL
COMPLEXITY
COULD OUTWEIGH THE BUSINESS
BENEFITS

Organizations grow in many ways: organically and quietly, organically and exponentially, by acquisitions or mergers, etc. In every step of growth there will always be more problems to solve. This will lead to more structures, processes and systems to address them and to cope with the new complexity.

At the beginning of the growth curve, the marginal gains of growth are worth that increased complexity. But at some point there will be a threshold beyond which, coping with the complexity starts to counterweigh the benefits (to be). There comes a time when the value of complexity may enter into the negative.

At that stage, it may be almost impossible to unbundle complexity and simplify the system, due to the nature of the interdependence of all of the components that the complexity has generated. Then rewinding is no longer an option.

Organizations only know one way to cope with this situation, which is to cut headcount, downsize, consolidate, shrink or whatever one wants to call it. But deleting nodes in the network of interdependent connections does not guarantee a smaller network. Indeed, that network may even collapse. It is like having a five star hotel and deciding to cut costs by closing half of the bedrooms whilst keeping the heating going, or closing down the kitchen and offering chocolate bars. The problem is having the five star hotel in the first place.

The Organizational Growth-Complexity Paradox that I have described above is my translation of Joseph Tainter's explanation of how complex societies collapse (*The Collapse of Complex Societies*, 1988). He said that societies such as the Roman Empire had a lot of sophistication, and that because of it, they could expand. They created more resources and built the mechanisms to cope with their management. In the case of the Romans, there were plenty of weaker territories to absorb, at least for a while. But that in itself became the problem: the management of complexity of communications, civil structures,

262

the military, etc. At some point, the system (the Empire) collapsed and split in two. The rest is history.

Incidentally, another way organizations cope with diminished returns in a stage of high complexity is the Roman Empire route: M&A.

Tainter went on to say that collapse was actually the best possible outcome for the Empire and not always bad for people. He quotes archaeological evidence showing that nutrition of individuals was better after the collapse than before.

Clay Shirky has also applied this concept to the collapse of complex business models, particularly in the digital world.

Organizational complexity is often seen as inevitable and part of growth itself. Sometimes it goes incredibly fast. Let's say we recruited 500 or 1000 new people in a short period of time. We have recruiting machineries and perhaps on-boarding ones, but it is not clear how, a few months down the road, we will deal with the liabilities of the complexity that this rapid hiring has generated. The same applies to M&A situations where the maths of 1+1= 2 doesn't work. 1+1= a Big 1. The 'Big 1' is a different beast that cannot be understood or managed as the simple sum of its parts.

Every successful growth contains the seeds of failure. So how we grow, matters. Recognizing the liabilities is the first step in gaining a healthy control of growth. But we also need a few vaccinations and safeguards. That, however, is the subject of another chapter.

There is nothing better to focus minds and show commitment than *The healing smell of a Corporate Bonfire.*

# THE LEGO AND THE JIGSAW: TWO WAYS TO BUILD AN ORGANIZATION

In the previous chapter, I said that successful growth contains the seeds of its failure. Managing the organizational complexity that has been created to cope with growth, may outweigh the benefits derived from growth itself. I said that emergency cost-cutting is hardly an answer and I compared it to owners of a five star hotel closing half of the bedrooms while keeping the heating on.

The way in which organizations grow matters. In what I call the 'Lego mode' of growth, organizations grow by adding more and more pieces all the time. If the Lego pieces are truly independent (as in the Lego system), there is always the possibility of reconfiguring the model by using the pieces somewhere else. These pieces are valuable in more than one place, they are transferable, they are re-assignable. The new model will look different, but most of the pieces will have been re-used. The big Lego model could also be split into smaller, equally meaningful Lego units, if this were needed to manage the business more efficiently.

In what I call the 'Jigsaw mode' of growth, the building pieces have a different role. They have a unique place in the model. They can't be reassigned to a smaller Jigsaw. Also, the Big Jigsaw cannot be downsized to a smaller one without losing its purpose and look. A piece lost or a piece out of place results in a gap, a hole. Getting rid of pieces in each quadrant of the Jigsaw, or a 10% 'reduction of pieces' across the board, will deliver an ugly Jigsaw with lots of holes.

Building Jigsaw organizations is exciting because everybody brought on board is unique, or a specialist, or 'just the piece we need'. However, the flexibility of the Jigsaw is very limited for the reasons I have explained above. Today, building Lego organizations with built-in reconfiguration capacity is a smart choice. Don't interpret this as forming a company of generalists. Lego organizations also contain 'unique people' and 'specialized' people, but the hiring is very mindful and highlights that they can be called upon to serve in different places, in different capacities and that the re-configuration is a strong possibility in any future.

The Jigsaw organization is highly specialized, but also highly inflexible. It can only be replaced with a different one. Read: start all over again.

A built-in capacity for reconfiguration and nurturing of the company memory (by at least avoiding the loss of knowledge through layoffs, which seems to be the norm in many reorganizations) are two design criteria to have in mind when building a new organization or growing an older one. There are other criteria that I use in my organizational architecture work, but these two are the ABC of modern company design.

The Lego and the Jigsaw represent two different views of the world, two different scripts and narratives and two different concepts of management and leadership.

266

# 'IT LOOKS LIKE A BELL CURVE. IT MUST BE AN HR PERFORMANCE APPRAISAL'. NOT IN THIS CENTURY. NORMAL DISTRIBUTIONS ARE DEAD.

Performance appraisal or performance management are one thing. Forcing Ranking into an artificial normal distribution of people in the organization is another. A Bell Curve (normal) distribution of performance is still used in many organizations. In this way of thinking (and it is a way of thinking) a majority of people will fall into the category of (average) contributors and, then, there will be a minority on one side (excellent performance, get the big bonus) and another minority on the other side (underperforming, on their way out). I am talking in caricature mode here, but anybody working in a medium to large organization will recognize this annual ritual, usually led by HR in order to 'classify people's performance'. Historically, it went as far as telling managers they must have so many in the mean area, so many in one standard deviation, so many in 2, etc. It was a 'you must have', not a 'what do you have?'

267

HR, but also leadership of organizations (we are all HR, not just aiming the shots at the HR function only) needed tools to classify people and trigger professional development, pay increase, bonus, etc. So for many years it was used as an intuitive and 'logic' tool, which then became ubiquitous.

However, the Bell Curve distribution in organizations is the wrong distribution for almost anything, even from a simple mathematical or statistical perspective. It is as irrelevant to organizations as it would be for supermarkets to explain their stocks in shelves. This is why.

The organization is a social network of connections. Bell Curves and social networks go together like oil and water. Most distributions in a network are not 'normal', but follow a Power Law/logarithmic distribution. In a Power Law distribution, a few have a lot of something (head), and most have fewer of something (long tail). For example: a relatively small number of people have high connectivity and influence and a relatively large number of people have low connectivity and influence. It works for connectivity on the web (relatively few sites, compared with the huge total, enjoy high connectivity; most sites enjoy low connectivity, as compared with the total) and in any social network (scale-free, it's the technical level). The organization IS a social network in which many dynamics (from connectivity to power) follow Power Law principles.

You may think that this can explain connectivity and influence (see my books *Viral Change* and *Homo Imitans*), but not necessarily performance. But the only reason why we think this way is because nobody has seriously thought about Power Law and performance. It is, however, logical that the distribution of 'performance' (which after all is not a single 'measure') follows the same rules as other true social network distributions. So imagine a top of 100 and a bottom of 0 and anything in between follows a power law/logarithmic distribution/curve. This is a much better representation.

The trouble is we are so used to Bell. The entire IQ system is based upon 100 being normal, 140 a genius and 60 a handicap. But this was merely a mathematical construct.

An additional problem is that HR/Bell/Force Ranking is heavily biased towards operational outcomes (read: hitting targets) and usually it says zero about other things such as connectivity, influence (positive or negative), positive deviance, experience, overall 'market value', etc. You are now going to tell me that Performance Management includes not only operational outcomes, but also values and 'soft stuff'. I see: 'Performance' as a conglomerate. When you give conglomerates a number (and a position in a curve) you risk falling into the phenomenon that I call 'Sumville'. This is a hypothetical town with a sign at its border: "Welcome to Sumville! Population: 2,500, 5 hotels, 20 pubs, 3 churches, 200 sheep. Total: 2,728'. For the record, I invented Sumville , but I have seen that sign.

None of my (serious) clients use Bell/Force ranking anymore. It is an artificial distribution. A broader problem, however, is a similarly artificial competence system, but this is a story for another day.

People's classifications are here to stay. It is in our nature to frame things (reality, concepts, people) to make sense of them. But many of our toolkits are old. The Bell Curve applied to people's performance creates more problems (including motivation and a high potential for unfairness) than it tries to solve. It is a convenient management tool, but in 2015 it's only justifiable as a means to provide convenience to management.

# MOBILIZING
## AND ENGAGING
## PEOPLE
### EMPLOYEE ENGAGEMENT
### MODELS
## A COMPANY OF
# VOLUNTEERS

# TWO WRONG TALENT WARS

**The war on talent.** McKinsey consultants started it with a book of the same title. By focusing on what seemed like a universal problem of scarce talent and a subsequent call to arms to acquire it, they skillfully managed to distract attention from a significantly greater problem: hosting talent. The military analogy (that management loves with narratives such as 'win-win' or 'kill the competition', for example) implies that talent is 'outside' and therefore there is a war to 'get it'. Undoubtedly true on some occasions, but organizations today have a greater problem with retention, engagement and, as I said, hosting that talent. If you fancy a war, it should be a war on employee engagement.

**The wrong capital.** 'Talent management' (a sub-industry in its own right) focuses too much on Human Capital, with emphasis on skills (and with emphasis on people 'who have done it before'). However, organizations are desperate for people with Social Capital (= quantity and quality of relationships) and people with Emotional Capital (= ability to understand and play with the soft, non-rational side of human behaviour). Of course, skills and capabilities are at the core of Talent

273

Management and rightly so. But I have not seen many Talent Management programmes paying much attention to the ability to master both relationships and emotions. Highly talented people with high IQs may have the social skills of a cactus! Just maybe. IQ is OK, but the trick is how to really master EQ (Emotional Intelligence) and SQ (Social Intelligence).

The best thing a Talent Management programme can do is to start by defining what 'talent' is.

You'd be surprised how many people can't seriously articulate this. And the narrower the definition (e.g. career progression), the bigger the problem.

# EMOTIONAL IGNORANCE NEEDS A BOOK

Emotional Intelligence was a 1-paragraph-length concept expressed in a library of publications. At the time it was a shock to the system. Do you really mean emotions count in hard management and leadership? Wow!

The Emotional Intelligence industry (that created subsequent sequels in the form of social intelligence, even spiritual intelligence) has continued to warn about the need for 'broader intelligences', in plural. And there is a place for this!

But what really needs a book is Emotional Ignorance. Or maybe even two books, or... errr.

Day after day, we see people in high places oblivious to what is going on, on the human side of the organization: too complex, too 'soft', too distracting.

This kind of ignorance is not the worst, though. It is the ignorance manifested in those who think they have a high

275

Emotional score, but behave like blind men in the land of people dynamics. It's this ignorance that worries me: robotic management, robotic processes, robotic systems managed by people who want… innovation, entrepreneurship and risk taking.

# YOUR BRANDING DEPARTMENT IS YOUR ENTIRE WORKFORCE

Your workforce is your sales force, your PR department, your Reputation Management Group, your Brand Managers, your Advocacy Group. It may be obvious, but many companies still spend fortunes on External Communication Programmes that simply don't click with their internal 'employee engagement'. And what about employees and social media?

A report by the consulting firm Weber Shandwick shows that in a sample of 2,300 employees, a third posted messages about the company. 16% of those were negative. It may sound like a small proportion, but any negativity can spread very quickly virally.

The study defines an employee activist as *"an individual who draws visibility to their workplace, defends their employers from criticism and acts as an advocate, both online and off."* This is a common use of the word 'activist' in the organization, but one which I personally dislike because (1) its mainly focused on the outside world (advocacy of the company) and (2) it's mainly defensive. Our use of the term 'activist' in our Viral Change™ programmes has nothing to do with this. Activists for us are employees who take a voluntary role in shaping a culture through peer-to-peer conversations and actions, focused on a specific, small set of behaviours.

Externally, employees can be advocates, for sure. The question is, how is the company actively supporting (or not) this external (social) interaction? According to the study, about half of the employers in the survey provided tools and/or content for employees to use in the social media world; and about one third allowed use of social media tools at work.

A 2008 book by David Brain and Martin Thomas, entitled *Crowd Surfing*, described the 180-degree difference between Microsoft (blogging promoted, encouraged and 'un-managed') and Apple (blogging forbidden). Today, six years later, companies are more on the Microsoft side than on the Soviet style Apple one.

Today, branding, reputation, employee engagement, digital (social) strategies, external communications, internal communication, PR and corporate affairs (just a small list) is one single bundle. The boundaries are all blurred. Unfortunately, each of the above has its own department and tribe, who focus their attention on solving the dilemma: 'my role, your role'.

Branding today is either behavioural, or it isn't branding. It's about the collective behavioural DNA of the organization. This is what people see and live. Branding is not a set of guidelines around colours and shapes. PR is not broadcasting. All these 'functions' need to go back to the drawing board and define 'their department' as one composed of everybody on the payroll and beyond (suppliers, advisors, alliances). The individuals in the functions that understand this will have a great time re-inventing. The ones who don't will become redundant.

278

# IS EMPLOYEE ENGAGEMENT (REALLY) WHAT IS MEASURED BY EMPLOYEE ENGAGEMENT SURVEYS?

Engagement, retention, even activism... traditional models of employee engagement are getting a bit tired. They are starting to look the same, smell the same and feel the same.

There was a running joke amongst Psychology students many years ago. When they asked: *"What's intelligence?"* the answer was always: *"Whatever is being measured by intelligence tests."* We are running the same risk: employee engagement these days is whatever numbers come from Employee Engagement surveys. It's a growing industry. Executives of all sorts are asking their HR colleagues, *"Can we have one of these?"* Or perhaps even telling them, *"we must have one of these!"*

Who could argue against having 'some numbers' that tell you how employees feel? Ah! The fascination with numbers! And what do you do with them? Well, you try to make sense of them, which is usually translated into lots of presentations to several layers of management. And then? Well, you must do something about it, which is usually translated into more meetings about what to do. And then? Action plans. And then? Follow-up meetings. And then? Then, it will be time for another Employee Engagement Survey.

Believe me, I am far from cynical. I am simply describing an organizational ritual. And rituals have a key role in organizations. They tend to do some good: they can glue people together, align people, make collective sense of things, provide maps, boost a sense of belonging, etc. They are not that good for solving problems, though. It's better to have those numbers than not to have a clue about the climate of the company. The serious question is what to do with those numbers other than 'try to boost them'.

I wrote an article many years ago: *Prisoners of the numbers.* Reading it again now, I can see how frustrated I was seeing Boards fixated on managing Earnings per Share (EPS) and share

280

prices and not on managing the organization, the people, the purpose. Little has changed.

I very much welcome the sub-industry of Employee Engagement surveys, providing it's not all about number-management, the discussion of an up-and down-scale, and the comparison with a neighbour. Many tools provide excellent, beautiful, sophisticated and expensive answers to the wrong questions. I have yet to find an organization that defines engagement first and then creates its survey. Most I know 'use that survey'... Because they can.

Time to rethink?

# [11O]

# RECLAIMING A CONCEPT THAT WAS LOST IN THE BUSINESS ORGANIZATION: VOCATION

Vocation is often defined as 'a strong feeling or drive' to do something, a job, a career, an occupation; to dedicate one's life to an idea, a trade, a craft. Typically it is applied to professions such as teachers, nurses, doctors or religious positions. It is agreed, in general, that following your own vocation is fantastic, and that not being able to do so is a human failure, perhaps even a personal tragedy.

'Vocation' has Latin and then French roots. It means 'a calling', a 'summons'. It has a tremendous religious connotation, but today the concept is applied more widely.

Vocation is not the same as a profession. It's not the same as a job. Vocations may 'include' a job (exercised to fulfill that vocation). But jobs don't have to include a vocation. It is possible, indeed frequent, that people have a job that does not match their vocation or that may even be in contradiction to it. Like the son who has a vocation for the arts, but is persuaded by his father to take over a family business which has nothing do with the arts. The son may not lose his vocation, but he will probably experience frustration if he cannot fulfill it.

I think that in business, we don't talk enough about vocations. It's easier to ask somebody about his job, or about jobs he or she likes to do, than asking 'what's your vocation?' I've met many people who have even found this embarrassing, as if we, in business, shouldn't get into these nuances. A job is a job, a career a career and a title in the rank, a title in the rank. We don't ask a successful CEO 'what's your vocation?' Well, not often anyway.

But if we could (re) introduce the 'vocation' idea into our narratives, we would gain enormously. For example, I don't know of any Employee Engagement system (assessment, survey) that asks plain and simple: "*What's your vocation? And can you fulfill it in this job?*" (Oh, the surprises we might have!) We ask about job satisfaction, even happiness, but not vocation.

A working place where vocations can flourish will be a step ahead of the game in any Employee Engaging framework. It may not be possible, of course, to cater for all vocations of our employees. But that does not mean that we can ignore this extraordinary motivational force. Speaking the language of vocations gives permission and prompts us to consider this higher form of engagement and to accept and live with possible trade-offs in the cases where this vocation cannot be realized and fulfilled.

Our Employee Engagement frameworks are too mechanical. They speak the language of machinery, such as 'going the extra mile' or 'discretionary efforts'. Both concepts, well-intentioned as they may be, are horribly mechanistic: more energy, more efforts, more output. The 'happy-place/happy-employee = better output' is a sad view of human nature.

When you see vocations in action, you invariably see something else as well: happiness. I personally have never seen happier people than those who can fully exercise their vocations. And I know a lot of people.

Just trying a little bit harder to rescue the concept may help us to better understand the whole motivational enigma. The one that today is sadly dominated by a very poor input-output model.

# THE ULTIMATE FORM OF EMPLOYEE ENGAGEMENT IS A COMPANY OF VOLUNTEERS

Many years ago, I was told by somebody very close to the old Microsoft management, in Bill Gates' times, that they had a layer of around 70 VPs right below Gates, that people called 'The Volunteers'. They called them that because they had made so much money, that they didn't need to be there. If they were there and showed up every day, it was because they chose to be there; that is, they were 'volunteers'.

Since then, I have been using this metaphor to explain the ultimate goal of Employee Engagement. It does not get any better than aspiring to be 'a company of volunteers'. It's a powerful anchor. Some people may think that it is a bit naïve or unrealistic, but it draws the attention to what people's real authentic engagement may look like.

Not a long time ago, these ideas were dismissed by a senior HR person in one of my client engagements: *"Everybody is a volunteer; everybody has a choice, if they don't like it, they don't have to be here."* It sounded to me as if she was saying, *"Don't you see? This is not North Korea."* It was a facile, arrogant dismissal, and it totally missed the point...

Studying the dynamics of volunteer organizations should be part of the curriculum, formal or informal, instructional or 'real life', for anybody in leadership. All the ingredients of empowerment, motivation, collaboration, control and autonomy are often found very quickly in these organizations. They are very vivid. When I tried this with a UN Refugee Organization, I learnt how normal it was to run the NGO with little control at the top and full empowerment of people on the ground. They had no other choice! And they mastered that. Not the case for our standard business organizations!

More than once, I have suggested to leaders to literally embrace this as their number one Personal Goal. Explicitly, written down: *"I will lead a company of volunteers."*

Just the thinking behind this idea, the effort required to understand what it would take, what would need to change, what the barriers would be to this company of volunteers, what 'employee engagement' might mean and what that organization might ultimately look like, is well worth the effort. Imagine it! I suggest you try it.

# [112]

# DEAR BUSINESS DEVELOPMENT CANDIDATE, TELL ME ABOUT THE THINGS YOU HAVE DEVELOPED **IN LIFE**

If you have a behaviour/value system and you want to recruit people while taking this value system into consideration, and if we take the well-established principle that the strongest prediction of future behaviour is past behaviour, then crafting the questions you will ask at an interview is a crucial task. This 'behavioural recruitment' is not new, but it is often poorly executed.

There are books and guidelines on how to create the right set of questions, but the crucial point is how to use those 'obvious questions'. For example, one website (of the very many that you will find by asking Mr Google) gives this question as an example: "*Give an example of how you set goals and achieve them.*" I've seen and used this (and many permutations of it) myself. The principle is sound. If one can't give an example of this, it would be fair to be 'suspicious'. But more often than not, people will give you an answer. However, with no other qualifications, chances are that people will give an answer relating to their previous job or the one before that. It is a predictable, contextual answer.

When you are applying for a Business Development job, you will probably give an example of what you've done as Business Development head in your current company (the one you are about to leave) or the previous one, perhaps, where you were Head of Marketing. It is all neatly linked, a continuous narrative of achievement geared towards giving the interviewer the comfort she seems to be asking for. Not difficult. And there's nothing wrong with that.

I am far more interested in the 'de-contextual' questions and answers. The non-Business Development context in the above case. Things that have to do, perhaps, with life outside work: social life, community life, etc. These are stronger questions as predictors because they tap deeper into the character of the individual as a whole. They tell you more about possibilities, drivers and hidden skills of the person, which the proposed working environment may make use of or enhance.

A good example is something that happened at Google at a time when 'cloning engineers' had reached a level of proficiency. But Google needed more than that. In fact, Google was fast progressing towards social connectivity and social networking, not just 'search'. I am conscious that I am using this historical remark as a bit of a caricature. Google wanted to hire people who understood 'social', who understood 'putting people together'. In that context, the questions were of the type: "*Tell us something you've done in high school that shows that you put people together, perhaps created a club, or led a community, or made people join in towards a common goal.*" Google was not going to create clubs or communities in that sense, but having that skill in your pedigree was thought to be a good predictor of 'understanding social'. The Masters Degree in Computer Sciences was the foot in the door; the genuine community organizer was the real qualification.

A good behavioural interview must have 'contextual' and 'de-contextual' questions. These questions may be the same, but the predictive value may be different. It should not be difficult to craft the questions associated with a value system and then think of scenarios outside the work context that one should explore. For example, if you are looking for accountability, stories of having been accountable in the previous job should bear less weight than stories of taking accountability in multiple life situations. Personally, I am more interested and place more weight on the latter.

One of the (in my opinion overplayed criticisms of behavioural recruitment when associated with a value or behavioural system, is that it runs the risk of creating clones. The 'de-contextual questions' that I am proposing, lower this risk a lot since they will point you in the direction of the 'deep character of the individual', not in the direction of somebody with a carbon copy set of skills looking for a set of boxes to tick.

# THE BEST EMPLOYEE RETENTION POLICY: 'I'LL PAY YOU TO QUIT!'

It's in the news! It's all over the place, particularly in mainstream US news: Amazon is paying employees to quit! If you are hesitating and you need a little nudge, Amazon would prefer you to leave and will give you a nice incentive in the form of some cash. Those 5,000 dollars may be just what will make you decide. Amazon needs the emotional attachment of its employees and if 5,000 dollars is enough to make you jump ship, then it's not worth keeping you.

The Pay to Quit policy was copied from Zappos (from the Spanish zapatos, for shoes), a company Amazon acquired in 2009. Zappos has a policy called 'The Offer'. Yes, once a year they give you the option to go and will pay you if you do. Zappos is a model of innovation for multiple things: it's a gigantic showcase full of surprises, a place of maximum employee engagement where happiness is more important than the zapatos. 'The Offer' is just another piece of their neat DNA.

It's not a major breakthrough to believe that hanging around in a company with little emotional attachment or engagement, is good for anybody. However, how many employee retention policies, including stock options, produce the opposite? Or heavily incentivize hanging around and waiting for a redundancy package.

Zappos is so incredibly proud of the commitment of its workforce that they can't afford to have people just hanging around. If The Offer is good enough to make you go, then Zappos is not the place for you.

When Amazon bought Zappos, they did so, not because they needed to sell more zapatos, but because Bezos knew what he was doing.

292

# BUILD YOUR OWN EMPLOYEE ENGAGEMENT ARGUMENT FOR FREE. YOU CAN'T GO WRONG.

Here are three baskets full of concepts:

Basket one: Working conditions, flexibility at work, pay and perks, reward and recognition, empowerment, good communication, people development plans, talent management, clear vision and purpose, internal digital connections, gamification and health & wellbeing programme.

Here is basket 2: Satisfaction, happiness, engagement, fun, self-belief, realization, enhancement, fulfilment and motivation.

And finally, basket 3: profitability, higher EPS, retention, reputation, customer satisfaction, loyalty, employer of choice, low absenteeism, safety, high quality and resilience in adversity.

Pick one concept from basket 1, say that it produces something from basket 2 (pick any concept there), which in turn, delivers something from basket 3 (pick one or two). You can't go wrong. And I bet you will always find some data to support the correlations between the items from the various baskets. Flexibility at work (basket one) creates high motivation (basket two) which leads to low absenteeism. Come on, give it a try. The combinations are great.

Constructing Employee Engagement arguments is not difficult at all. There are always correlations between items from basket 1 and 3, or 1 and 2, or 2 and 3, etc. The problem is these are simply correlations. The connections aren't (always) based on causality.

Most Employee Engagement arguments that we use in organizations are semi-rich in correlations and very weak in causality. The truth is that it is hard to tell, for example, whether satisfaction delivers profitability, or profitability delivers satisfaction. The fact that we may see both going hand in hand does not make the one-directional causal argument true.

Many Employee Engagement systems and questionnaires are based upon the assumption of something from conceptual basket one, delivering something from basket two and/or three. We have taken the argument at face value. We have converted correlation into causality.

But as the Spurious Correlations website reminds us, there is also a strong correlation between the per capita consumption of mozzarella cheese in the USA and the number of civil engineering doctorates awarded. Or between the divorce rate in the state of Maine and the per capita consumption of margarine.

While most sensible people would not infer that feeding your son mozzarella cheese will make it highly probable that he will get a Civil Engineering doctorate, or that banning margarine would work miracles for decreasing the divorce rate in Maine, many managers would be very happy to declare the correlation between anything in basket one with anything in basket two and/or three a true causal chain of events. The whole industry of Employee Engagement is based upon this.

When I show these arguments to large audiences in my speaking engagements, I get the whole spectrum of reactions. The data-fundamentalists get very irritated, despite the fact that they can't really show serious data to prove causality. The 'Employee Engagement people', equipped with all their questionnaires, get even more irritated. The Cynical contingency says that what I am inferring is that we should not do anything, not bother at all about Employee Engagement initiatives, because all data is flawed.

But the latter is far from my position. I think we should do anything we believe will improve the company, period. It's called Good Management and I am all for it. But managers need to use more rigorous critical thinking. Do as much as needed for good management and avoid the simplistic causal interpretation of input-output: if we do more Town Hall meetings with all employees, it will give them more 'voice' and air time, it will improve their morale and that will increase performance. The company is not an input-output machine. For goodness sake, let's do what we believe we need to do without the constant need to justify the output! Maybe it is simply morally good, managerially sound and probably beneficial for the mental health of all to give employees more airtime, more voice, more say and a more proactive role. Why do you then need a score in a questionnaire to tell you that you should do that?

By the way, here is another one: the number of films in which Nicolas Cage appeared, correlated highly with the number of people drowned by falling into a swimming pool. He should really stop his movie career, or else we will have to make fences around pools compulsory.

# [115]

# THE SHORTEST EMPLOYEE ENGAGEMENT SURVEY HAS ONE QUESTION...

And the question is: "*Why are you still here?*"

You learn about the organization by asking employees questions when they leave (exit interviews), but you can learn far more when you ask them why they are staying ('stay' interviews). It's not a joke. "*Why are you still here?*" – with the emphasis on the word still – is the best Employee Engagement survey you can have. It's also very cheap and you don't need an external agency.

It's the only question that allows the person to respond with something like "*I need to pay my mortgage*" (I have never seen an Employee Engagement survey with this kind of answer). Also, possibly, "It's the best place I could dream of working in", and anything in between. We are so afraid of direct questions that we tend to ask people things in complicated ways. I have practiced this with clients many times and I always got the richest of answers. Believe me, a one-question questionnaire is a dream.

296

# DEBUNKING THE MYTHS OF EMPLOYEE ENGAGEMENT.
## A LAND OF EMPERORS WITHOUT CLOTHES
## THE SIX MODELS

Employee engagement has become an industry in its own right and it is taking over a lot of airtime. I want to 'elevate the confusion to a higher level'. Not really! But I think anyone in the Human Capital business should put their cards on the table. A bit risky, though. Some truths may make us uncomfortable. I hope that many friends will still be friends after this miniseries starting today. There are many Emperors without clothes out there who may catch a cold!

Today I will lay out the six frameworks that are out there, one way or another, competing with each other in the area of Employee Engagement. These are the six models that I have run into in my research and consulting practice:

1. 'Air time': This is a 'voice model'. Employees are informed and also listened to. A dialogue is supposed to be established.

What 'they' say counts. Management listens to 'them'. Surveys and rankings dominate this model. The measurement tools tend to take over the narrative. 'Employee voice' acquires a jargon of its own. 'Giving voice' seems to be the aim, more than a clear idea of what to do with that voice. It looks like surveys and Town Halls.

2. 'Happy Cows'. I did not invent the term! There is a book with the title: *Contented cows* (employees) *give better milk* (productivity). This is a machine model. Provide good input, you'll get a good output. Employee happiness and satisfaction will deliver better results. The machine is oiled with good working conditions and rewards. Cows are happy, milk is good. The whole employee satisfaction and 'happiness industry' sits here. This is an input/output model. Narratives such as 'the extra mile' and 'discretional effort' sit here.

3. 'Cause'. Employees are engaged <u>within</u> the company in noble causes that the company either has or adopts. It's often an 'NGO inside' model. People's engagement provides meaning, sense of worth and the glue for the cohesion of the organization. And this is good for everybody. Bring green and sustainability stuff inside, engage the employees and voila!! You have 'employee engagement'. Entire NGO businesses are sponsored by Big Consultancies and Big Companies as a means to 'bring the cause inside' and provide 'engagement glue' for employees. It's a lucrative business.

4. 'The Investors metaphor'. In this model, the employee is an investor of his/her own human capital in the organization. At year-end, there is either good or bad outcome! HR people and management are 'Human Capital Investment Fund Managers'. This is an underestimated model. It gives power to the employee, as an 'investor'. This model had a timid attempt at getting off the ground a few years ago, but since then it has lost some steam. It's a bit of a revolutionary gem in the making. But the wait for it to take off is longer than one may have expected at the beginning. It tells us that 'employee power' is still low.

298

5. 'Moral Drive'. Employee engagement exists… because it's morally good, regardless. Commitment has to do with human dignity and the power of work is a means to the enhancement of the individual. Don't look for reference to this in an MBA curriculum. But you can find some inspiration in the Catholic Social Teaching documents. Few people may identify with this as a model of any kind. After all, some people say organizations and businesses are 'amoral'. Darwinian capitalism has a bit of a laugh with this model. Moral what?

6. 'Activism'. Employees take charge in a progressive, self-managed way. They are active in a peer-to-peer environment. They are engaged <u>with</u> the company not just <u>within</u> the company. Doing is greater than talking or advocating. Activists do. 'Act' is part of this word. They figure out what to do and how. Then they do it. Leadership gains control by losing control. This model states that 'the ultimate goal of employee engagement is self-management'. This concept of 'activism' has little to do with the one used by the consultancy Weber Shandwick (*Employees Rising: Seizing the Opportunity in Employee Activism*) which proposes to convert the employees into 'Brand Advocates'.

First port of reflection: where are you on this scale? Which model(s) represent(s) engagement within your organization? It's bound to be a mixture, but, can you recognize these models?

[117]

DEBUNKING THE MYTHS OF EMPLOYEE ENGAGEMENT.

# MODEL 1:
# 'AIR TIME'
## GIVING EMPLOYEES A VOICE.

SO NOW WE HAVE A CHOIR. NOW WHAT?

Model 1 of my 6 is what I call, 'Air time'. It translates into: "*We recognize that employees' views are not properly heard; employees need a voice.*" And I'm not talking Unions here.

Model 1 usually comes disguised as one of two solutions:

**Solution one:** we will go around the sites and affiliates and will organize lots of Town Hall Meetings, Executive Road-shows, All-Hands-On-Deck meetings, etc. (Sometimes it's funny to hear this because the planning of actions seems to be about giving more voice to management than to employees. But of course there will be a big Q&A at the end.)

*Scenario A:* following the 250 PowerPoint slides, management is seriously puzzled because there are hardly any questions. "*They don't ask anything!*"

*Scenario B:* there are questions by two people who express incredibly negative views. These dominate all the Q&A airtime and people go back to their offices with negativity reinforced ("*be careful what you ask for, you might get it*".)

Tip: holding Town Hall meetings and ending up reinforcing negative feelings is stupid and worse than not doing Town Halls at all.

*Scenario 3:* Everything goes well, there is a reasonable dialogue and everybody feels good.

**Solution two**: we do an Employee Engagement/Employee Satisfaction/Climate survey. Giving voice? Yes, sure, here is the questionnaire. As we all know, there is a whole industry here. Survey is done, Gantt charts are displayed, and numbers find a home in spreadsheets... but there are these little red asterisks at the end of the bars that say that your division is below average. Not good. Emergency Management Team meeting dictates that we need to tackle those little red asterisks. Particularly the ones that say that people do not feel heard. We must give more voice to people: go to Solution one. For the rest of the asterisks, we will create lots of mandatory workshops to find solutions, and each sub-management team will report back (mandatorily).

Ok, but what about this 'Air Time' model?

**Pros.** Increasing employee voice and giving employees more air time is much better than (a) the absence of either or (b) a poor state of affairs in this area.

**Cons**. When implemented as a tick-box exercise, it's a complete waste of time and energy, a lost opportunity and, in some cases, an insult and source of further disengagement. Employee Surveys are often executed as an annual or bi-annual ritual, something to go through, and something that triggers 'actions' to show that we listen to employees, that 'they' have a voice. I have often asked: *"Why do you do an employee survey?"* and more than once have been told: *"because the Board wants one!"*

**So what?** When Model 1, 'Air Time', is used in isolation, it's hardly a solution to anything. It does not mean that some people won't like it or won't be grateful. However, 'Model 1' used in isolation, can have the opposite effect from what was intended, and is often a bit of corporate exhibitionism. Model 1 makes sense when it is not the only model in town, when it's part of a wider and more mature engagement plan. Trouble is, many Employee Engagement programmes in organizations are full-blown 'Model 1 only'.

DEBUNKING THE MYTHS OF EMPLOYEE ENGAGEMENT.

# MODEL 2:
# 'HAPPY COWS'
HAPPY COWS GIVE BETTER MILK.

There is a book or two and the associated speeches/ workshops/websites, all under the title *Contented Cows still (give) better milk*. OK. It's a book about Employee Engagement. The book also holds a place on some lists of Leadership Development books. I don't imagine it's about the development of cows, but who knows?

Leaving the amusing concept and the great marketing mind of the authors (even the book) aside, conceptually, this model is alive and well although many people would prefer to avoid the bovine analogy. Beyond the cows, this is an input/output model. If we feed the cows (sorry) well enough, they will be happy and will give better milk (the reviews emphasize the distinction between happy and contented, just in case you wanted to add some philosophical depth). Simple. Find out what makes the cows happy and off we go. Flexible time, good pay and incentives, table tennis, good cafeteria (cows will give seriously worse milk if you keep those vending machines), working from home, dress-down Fridays, company barbeques, maternity leave and points to buy goods online. There are about 1,000 other things. You won't be short of food for 'happiness'.

This model is that of a machine. Use good oil and you'll see how well it works. We can make as much fun as we like of the analogy (and I for one am very grateful to the authors for their imagination and for the many wonderful conversations in the corridor with clients when I mention this), but there is a whole Employee Engagement sub-industry that, while it may not use the bovine analogy, it uses the same principles. Words such as 'employee satisfaction', 'happiness', etc. are used here. The whole narrative of 'going the extra mile' (when more gas has been added) and 'discretionary effort', so intrinsic to traditional HR/Employee Engagement models, belongs here.

**Pros.** Well, the title is funny and you'll remember the model.

**Cons.** Err, small detail, people are not machines, but, hey, we have been using machinery language for a long time.

**So what?** What is wrong with flexible time, good pay and incentives, table tennis, a good cafeteria, working from home, etc.? Absolutely nothing! The difference lies in how you treat these. Are they good in their own right, contributing to a favourable environment, or are they cynical tools to feed the cows? If you knew that your cows (here we go again) were already happy, would you bother to add all these 'benefits'?

Are you providing flexible time for young mothers because you think that young mothers need flexible time or because you have many young mothers (and fathers) employed and the increased flexible time correlates with 2 points up in the Employee Engagement Survey?

**PS:** This model of Employee Engagement was first described as 'Panem et Circenses' in AD 100 by Juvenal. Its translation is 'Bread and Circuses' and it described how Roman Emperors kept the masses happy (sorry, contented) with entertainment and food. And the Roman masses would go the extra mile and provide discretionary effort. Well, at least until the Visigoths decided to visit.

# 119

DEBUNKING THE MYTHS OF EMPLOYEE ENGAGEMENT.

# MODEL 3:
# 'THE CAUSE'
ENGAGEMENT **WITH** THE COMPANY
OR **WITHIN** THE COMPANY?

Employees join forces to work on a Cause: green agenda, corporate responsibility, a local or global NGO, a civic or societal Cause. The Cause acts as the glue. Cross-collaboration is boosted. An enhanced sense of worth, of noble collective aim is in the air. Activities take place. The internal (and external) marketing of the Cause is very visible. There may be a collective sense of excitement. Great initiative. Most people approve.

Years ago, I naively asked a friend who runs a very successful international NGO in the anti-pollution (plastics) area, where he got the money from. The answer was dead-pan and given to me with a 'don't-you-get-it?' look: *"Corporate!"* I continued to make a fool of myself by asking what on earth 'Corporate' could gain from sponsoring (obviously this is not pocket change) a Non-Governmental Organization in the anti-plastic area, unless they themselves where in the same area. E.g. they were potential polluters and committed to change, so they asked for his help; or they were also organizations similarly working towards the anti-pollution goals. Surely this is what he meant. He gave me a second 'you-still-don't-get-it?' look and produced a second statement, this time louder: *"Employee Engagement!"*

*"Please explain,"* I begged. *"Well, having the workforce engaged in my NGO activities, many of which take place inside the firm, boosts employee engagement in the company and the Employee Engagement survey scores go up, by a lot. This is worth a lot of money to them."* I asked for an example of 'them'. I was expecting (again, still a bit foolishly) a major polluter or a business with challenging waste management operations. However, he gave me the name of a Big Consulting Firm whose pollution capacity was only possibly related to the amount of air-miles accumulated by its workforce.

At the time, I did not see the point in continuing that conversation about whether being engaged <u>within</u> the company was or was not the same as being engaged <u>with</u> the company (a distinction provided by my always very perceptive partner and colleague, Caroline Tierney). But this distinction is key.

**Pros.** There is nothing intrinsically wrong with employees being engaged <u>within</u> the company on an external cause. On the contrary, I think this is great.

**Cons.** The 'NGO-inside' model, mobilizing as it may be, cannot be seen as the same as engagement <u>with</u> the company's own aims and vision. Taken to the extreme, this is just another, more sophisticated version of model 2, 'Happy Cows' (Panem et Circenses). It may miss the point completely, although people may become very engaged indeed, with the anti-pollution idea.

**So what?** It's a question of honesty marrying clarity. When you can marry both societal aims and your own operations, there is clearly a win-win. A good example is the British retailer Marks & Spencer and their 'Plan A' (Why Plan A, people ask? Because there is no plan B, they say). The website says: *"Plan A is a journey towards becoming the world's most sustainable retailer... and we're proud of the awards we're winning along the way."*

They have a series of public commitments in the areas of recycling, waste management, carbon trust, etc. I am not quoting M&S from a position of authority on these matters (my authority on the matter is zero), but as an example of what seems to be a blend of true employee engagement, 'The Cause' model and the company's operational objectives.

The world is full of companies offering time for volunteer work, sponsoring great causes and expressing big Corporate Social Responsibility aims. And many people say that these <u>are</u> Employee Engagement.

308

I suspect, however, that much of this is engagement of employees with noble activities. I would suspend judgment as to whether all of them are engaged with the company. I don't believe for a second that both engagement within the company and engagement with the company are always the same.

# 120

DEBUNKING THE MYTHS OF EMPLOYEE ENGAGEMENT.

# MODEL 4: 'THE INVESTORS METAPHOR'

EMPLOYEES AS INVESTORS OF THEIR OWN (HUMAN) CAPITAL

This is model 4 of the series. The concept is simple. Imagine that you, as an employee, are in reality an investor. Not of money, but of another form of capital: your own human (intellectual and time) capital. The employer pays you for the use of that capital with a promise to grow it. Employers are Intellectual Capital Fund Managers.

Good Fund Managers will deliver good returns. At the end of the year you should expect a return on the (human) capital that has been invested: better skills, personal and professional enhancement, greater 'market value' and 'market-ability', more knowledge, new experiences... You define your expected returns. After all, you are the investor.

Nobody (invests) gives capital to Fund Managers with a poor track record. You should not expect a year-end without growth or indeed, loss of capital! The deal with your employer is that the contract is for the use and growth of your Human Capital. So, the one who is really in charge here is actually you. Novel concept. HR departments become 'Human Capital Investment Fund Brokers'. The company is a big investment fund.

The idea is old and I have written about this several times before, for example in *Disruptive Ideas*. For various reasons, it has not obtained great visibility.

There is a connection here with *The Alliance* by Reid Hoffman, Ben Casnocha and Chris Yeh. These authors propose an employee-employer 'contract' with mutually beneficial rules of the game over an agreed period of time (not a forever relationship) that they baptized 'Tour of Duty' (which I think is an unfortunate name). But these 'Tours of Duty' are not the same as the relationships in the 'Investors Metaphor'.

**Pros.** The Investors metaphor model is a smart way to reposition the power of the employee. Engagement is high! How could it be otherwise if you are the investor? Why would you invest in a mediocre way or put in half-hearted effort?

**Cons**. It's highly disruptive in terms of organizational models. Companies may be shouting at you: *"Investor in what?"* In my own client work, I have seen reactions to this of the type: *"Interesting!"* which is an English expression that translates into anything from *"I don't believe you"* to *"Nonsense!"*, but never, ever truly into actually 'interesting'). Proponents of the 'Built to last' old school of thinking are restless about models that don't shoot for long(er) term stability. The 'Investors Metaphor' may seem like one of these, but it's not. You'll invest for as long as (a) you have something to invest (so if you are poor in Human Capital, or becoming poorer, you have a problem) and (b) the return on your investment is worth it.

**So what?** The 'Investors Metaphor' makes you think. A lot. It's a legitimate model of employee engagement, although hardly ever referred to. Use it in combination with other ingredients and the cooking looks (and smells) promising.

DEBUNKING THE MYTHS OF EMPLOYEE ENGAGEMENT.

# MODEL 5:
# 'THE MORAL IMPERATIVE'
## THE FORGOTTEN MODEL

Here is a 'very novel' concept. Employee Engagement is needed because... it's good in and of itself. Because work enhances human nature. Because engaging people with their work is a moral obligation of both providers and takers of work, it is part of human enhancement. In this model, meaningful, enhancing enrichment from work is a moral imperative. If engagement is morally right, it also means that work matters to the individual beyond the benefit of the organization. Full stop.

This thinking is so alien to business that it's likely to be dismissed by many. After all, many people maintain that the organization per se, and in particular the business organization, is an amoral entity. It has undergone moral surgery. Its imperative is not to deal with any morality other than the purpose of the firm and the goals of the owners. Shareholder value is shareholder value. If the firm has a value system, it's up to management to figure out how to increase that shareholder value within the corporate value frame. Employee/people's enhancement as human beings, in this thinking, is neither here nor there, unless expressed specifically in relation to the value system itself.

For people who don't ascribe to this model, the above statement 'engaging people with their work is a moral obligation as part of creating human enhancement' is a leftist fairy tale.

The 'ethics of work' (not the same as the ethics of business) is not precisely a new topic. It's just that business organizations are busy 'making other plans' (as in John Lennon's "*Life is what happens to you while you're busy making other plans*"").

We have three strong pillars in our modern history:

(1) Max Weber's *The Protestant Ethic*.

(2) The Catholic Social Teachings, a scattered series of documents with detailed development on seven principles:

314

Life and the dignity of the human person;
Call to family, community and participation;
Solidarity;
Dignity of work;
Rights and responsibilities;
Options for the poor and vulnerable; and
Care for God's creation.

Most of them address 'work' one way or another.

(3) The Right to Work is treasured within the Universal Declaration of Human Rights.

These three pillars have both followers and critics.

**Pros**. The model brings back some conversation about 'purpose', to which people may agree or disagree, but still, the conversation will be in the air. With my clients, I still use a lecture from 1990 by the great Charles Handy, with the title *What is a company for?*, which challenged many assumptions at the time and which continues to be relevant today.

**Cons**. It's hard to bring up this conversation in the context of 'busy people making other plans'. But, if we can have a Cow Model (number 2) I don't see why we could not have a Moral model.

**So what?** Purpose is back, it's the new black. Purpose is not the same as 'Employee Engagement as moral imperative', but they are sisters. This model says: when you look at all models, all possibilities, all surveys, all rankings, all happy cows, all air time, could you slot in a possibility that work in itself should be enhancing? And the corollary: if this is the case, then management needs to look at employee engagement as employee enhancement as well.

What if we added a moral obligation here, in this model?
Would the sky fall?

DEBUNKING THE MYTHS OF EMPLOYEE ENGAGEMENT.

# MODEL 6:
# 'ACTIVISTS ON THE PAYROLL'
## (WITH THE COMPANY ENGAGEMENT)

In this model, the employee is (1) an activist, (2) largely working peer-to-peer and (3) progressing towards (if not arriving at) self-management. Let me qualify the three components:

1) Activist. This means to act. The word activist contains the word act. This is activism both <u>within</u> the company and <u>with</u> the company. The cause (model 3) is the company's cause, not somebody else's or that of an adopted NGO. But activist (act) is not the same as Advocate (endorse). Using employees as advocates for the reputation of the company and calling them activists is flawed.

In this model, activist is another name for employee. Empowerment is a redundant word. Everybody on the payroll is de facto empowered.

(2) Peer-to-peer. Work is organized (and most likely self-organized, although there may be different degrees within the company) as peer activity. The unit of work may be two or three people. Most progress (planning, decisions, operations, control) is bottom-up. There is a top-down, well-defined framework and well-orchestrated Backstage Leadership™ that supports and enables (without hindering) the work through peer-to-peer networks.

(3) Self-management as a destination. I've written before that the self-management train has left the station. The employee as an activist is a necessary ingredient. In this model there is little 'permission' required from people before people can take action. There are no Ambassadors (people representing others), everybody represents him or herself.

**Pros.** The model has the highest potential for employee engagement, since this bottom-up, grassroots-driven, progressively self-managed and supported by Backstage Leadership™ workforce contains most components for such engagement both 'with' and 'within' the company.

317

**Cons**. Many people consider these approaches as only applicable to selected types of companies and industries. Many publicized examples of organizations navigating these waters are of forward thinking software companies, which does not help in convincing 'harder industries' that the principals may be equally relevant.

**So what?** Here in this model, readers may identify the spirit of Viral Change™. It would be pointless for me to be apologetic for my preferences!

These models are proposed here as tools, as bricks to build a house, not as pieces of dogma. It is perfectly reasonable to see 'all of the above' in one organization, to differing degrees. But there are choices to be made. For example, if employee engagement is mainly biased towards model 1 or 'Air time', the organization will look, feel and smell very different from organizations with another focus or indeed, a combination of foci.

These Six Lego Pieces of Engagement, on their own or in combination, will lead you to very different lands.

# CHANGE, THE BIG WORD

## RESISTANCE, CORPORATE REVOLUTIONS, KOTTER'S OLD STEPS,

## BOTTOM-UP CHANGE
### (WHEN NECESSARY, USE WORDS)

# JOHN KOTTER'S 8-STEP CHANGE MANAGEMENT MODEL IS THE BEST CHANGE MODEL OF THE LAST CENTURY.

WHY IT IS STILL ALIVE IN 2014 IS BEYOND ME.

John Kotter, Harvard professor Emeritus and prolific author, has made a significant contribution to Leadership and Change for many years. In Change Management, he has brought order to an area that was in need of structure. His 8-step model is now a ubiquitous piece in teaching, consulting and writing. As many people would agree, it is a classic text used in most Business Schools. Indeed, many professionals would equate 'Kotter' to 'Change'.

The language of the 8 steps has penetrated everywhere, providing a recipe for how to transform organizations, how to 'do' change management and, not a small thing, how to create a consulting business backed by the Kotter/ Harvard pedigree.

The 8-step model is neat, elegant, simple, rational, memorable, saleable and immensely out of date.

But who would disagree with the rationality of:

> Establishing a sense of urgency
> Forming a powerful guiding coalition
> Creating a vision
> Communicating a vision
> Empowering others to act on the vision
> Planning for and creating short-term wins
> Consolidating improvements and producing even more change
> Institutionalizing new approaches.

I don't know if Kotter thinks of these as truly sequential, although the fact that he calls them 'steps' makes me think he does. I challenge anybody to explain to me how you successfully implement this model today, in this sequence, in any organization.

The linear, sequential world has gone. We can't wait for a sense of urgency to penetrate throughout the organization before we act. The Guiding Coalition, if hierarchical, has less power than a bottom-up or grassroots system. The vision today is never a completely formed 'step'; it's evolving all the time.

Communicating to all 'using every possible vehicle', as stated, implies top-down communication, which fails to deliver 70% of the time. Empowering others and 'encouraging risk' implies that this is 'granted' by the leadership. But today, this is mainly behavioural, not a concession received and the model does not account for this. Planning for and creating short-term wins: sure. But many organizations stay in the 'short-term, quick wins' mode for the long term. Consolidating assumes reaching a point of stability. Stability? What is that? Institutionalizing new approaches. Ah! So the New Promised Land has been reached.

I am fully conscious that I am caricaturizing the model, but I don't believe I have ventured too far from its essence. Again, it all may have made sense in the last Century, but not in the 21st Century. A long time ago, though I think it was still in this century, I wrote that I would have less of a problem with Kotter's model if we were to apply the Woody Allen reference: "*all seasons in one afternoon*" (when talking about the weather in London). Kotter's steps, mixed up and active 'all at the same time' may make a bit of sense, although the model fails to point out the Elephant in the Room in many organizations, i.e. Behaviours.

Top-down, linear, rational, communications-driven change management projects fail at a rate close to 80%. They all have Kotter genes.

It would be unfair to leave this hanging on a note of criticism, so I will provide the alternative. Apologies, there is not much room here for a full articulation. Then again, no apologies, the rationale is fully articulated in my books *Homo Imitans* and *Viral Change*™.

So, for a quick summary here. Optimum organizational change and transformation today, including cultural transformation, is bottom-up, grassroots change (as opposed to top-down). It is behavioural based (as opposed to exclusively communications-based). Behaviours are spread and scaled up by peer-to-peer, internal social copying (an epidemic model, not information tsunami). The scale-up is driven by a small number of individuals who have little to do with the hierarchy of the system (the 'powerful coalition' is grassroots; these people need to be found, it's not a volunteering model). It's all cooked in the informal organization (as opposed to in teams and committees) and supported by a well-orchestrated storytelling system. Leadership is Backstage Leadership™: formal leadership supporting the real, distributed, grassroots leaders and shredding all of their PowerPoints.

And although there is some sequence in the above, it allows for quite a lot of parallel, emergent and simultaneous fires on the mountain.

The motto for the Kotter model is: *"Life is linear."*

The Viral Change™ motto is: *"Life is short."*

NOT EVEN BOTTOM-UP. CERTAINLY NOT TOP-DOWN. LASTING ORGANIZATIONAL CHANGE IS A POLYCENTRIC, SOCIAL MOVEMENT, OR IT ISN'T CHANGE.

In organizational life, we are used to the dichotomy 'top-down' and 'bottom-up', for example when we talk about change. Clearly, there is some truth to this. There is an assumption that if you want the opposite to top-down it has to be bottom-up. But in organizational terms, and even more as soon as you consider the organization as a social network, the true alternative to an exclusively top-down approach, which is uni-centric, is polycentric. (Exclusively bottom-up would be as unicentric or uni-directional as top-down.)

This is not just playing with words. It is significant. Successful political campaigns are poly-centric. The 2008 and 2012 Obama campaigns, for example, were ones with heavy emphasis on the grassroots 'centres'. The 'localized' number of these 'centres' was significantly greater than on the Republican side. But there were other 'centres': fundraising, central political party leadership, Senate and House members, etc. None of these 'centres' alone, working in isolation, would have led to victory.

Viral Change™ in organizations, which my team has pioneered, takes place by orchestrating a polycentric approach. With the organization as a pyramid (and it could be a big, steep pyramid or a flat(ter) pyramid), there are more highly connected and influent people in the bottom of that pyramid statistically. That is why a great majority of 'champions' or 'activists' come from the lower layers. But Viral Change™ takes place at different layers (to continue using a wrong two-dimensional concept) and 'designed' peer-to-peer activity (conversations, engagement, activists' role...) is also taking place at different layers and from different 'centres'. This is how a social movement works, whether it occurs spontaneously, or, very often, is truly orchestrated. Although the term grassroots is used (and we do use it as well, indeed), on its own it still gives a false sense of uni-direction.

In Viral Change™ we say that "*we orchestrate large scale behavioural change to create a social movement.*" Business

**326**

organizations may not be used to the term 'social movement', but this is what it is. I sometimes have a little bit of extra work to do explaining to clients what we mean by this. Still, 'social movement' is sometimes seen as something alien to the 'inside' of the organization, something more appropriate to what one sees on TV and in sociology books. But once explained the logic is powerful.

I understand that mobilizing people and creating 'a movement' – something that political and marketing campaigners do for a living – has not ranked very high in the organizational life or in management thinking. We need to change this. But we need a trans-disciplinary approach, as we have in Viral Change™. No single discipline can explain and master large organizational change today.

In our consulting work, when it comes to large-scale behavioural and cultural change, we have learnt more from the history of social movements and from the study of political campaigns, than from traditional 'management thinking'. Then add network theory, behavioural sciences and other key ingredients...

Certainly, 'social movement' was not a term to be found in any of my MBA materials, many moons ago.

# [125]

# CORPORATE NEEDS A 60S COUNTER-CULTURE REVOLUTION AND THESE ARE THE FIVE TRENDS THAT COULD DELIVER IT

The 60s was a counter-culture time of rapid change, whether you liked it or not, whether you lived through it or not. The only real analysis of that time could be retrospective and enough water has gone under the bridge to allow us to assess the ingredients: the Vietnam war, rejection of traditional authority, generation clashes, alternative lifestyles, race relationships in turmoil, experimentations in sexuality, drugs and a few other things. It was a package. Historians and social academics have analyzed it and will continue to do so. What everybody agrees on is that there was a 'catalytic moment' of rapid change, not a historical continuum. And the Beatles provided the soundtrack.

With my apologies to those who in the 60s were still in a state of 'potential concept' and perhaps only landed on earth later

328

thanks to 'Imagine', candles and red wine (not a comprehensive list of factors here).

There are always historical points of convergence, accumulation of factors that have the potential to create great discontinuity, as opposed to continuity. I believe the conditions are now here for a counter-culture revolution of the firm, the corporate world, the business organization.

I can't pretend to develop this argument in less than 1,000 words like in a PhD, so I will take the liberty of simply announcing the key ingredients. I don't know what the final dish will look like, but my hypothesis is that it will be something equivalent to the 60s counter-revolution, but this time for corporate life.

I believe there are five distinctive bundles, packages, groups of factors, Lego pieces for the revolution at hand. The combinations of facts may look like strange bedfellows. The concepts may be dismissed easily. The 'what's new?' brigade will sweep some of them under the carpet. Or all of the above. But here they are, as I see them:

1. Social purpose is not just a nice, theoretical, ethical, politically correct concept anymore. Millennials and others are actively seeking it, wanting to work for a company with 'this', buying products from purpose-driven producers and seriously believing profit is secondary to purpose. Enron was the inflection point. The banking crisis a reminder. In the quest for purpose, all professions, politicians, firms, current forms of organizations are on death row. If you think that purpose is the same as 'mission and vision', abandon the corporate Titanic now.

2. Taking control of one's destiny is serious. The Arab Spring and its summer and autumn, has shown that it is possible to join revolutions in real time. There is an

Arab Spring at hand in the corporate world. Forms and models of self-management in organizations have passed the anecdotal threshold to become more and more present in traditional industries. An 'Employee Revolution' will show up on a screen near you. That will make a historical, pre-Copernican footnote of the current 'Employee Engagement' thinking.

3. Digitalization is bigger than globalization. End of distance and end of space are not new, but they are now in full-blown use. The 24/7 ability to act destroys the 9-to-5 workday. Work-life balance is dead. People seek another form of life, not just a balance or imbalance. A sense of belonging, loyalty and 'engagement' is what they are looking for. The rules for how are not carved in stone.

4. New forms of work are ubiquitous, not anecdotal anymore. Full-time and part-time are old concepts. People are experimenting with shared work, shadow work, remote working, working anonymously. It's a big experiment and not all of it is good. Some glorified forms such as 'working from home' are simply emperors without clothes. Very traditional forms of work will learn to cohabit with very unusual forms of work. Learn leadership acrobatics now! Suspend judgment as to what may work. Experiment! ('Experiment' is a wonderful 60s counter-culture concept, so here we go again).

5. 'Built to last', to use the title of a prominent bestseller (better described as a business Bible), is dead. A tiny percentage of start-ups survive, but many resurrect in other forms. Some die again. It's continuous reincarnation. *"What would the magic bullets of long term success be?"* is the Holy Grail of corporate. A few Crusades are underway. People are very confused. The muddle is huge. In the short term, 'Build to think' is my

preferred mode. Taleb's *Antifragile* (2012) is ahead of the game.

All that put together has the potential of a counter-revolution in the making. All the ingredients are available in your local cultural supermarket. The question is whether you want to wait for an invitation to dinner or if you prefer to find yourself in the kitchen. For the record, I am cooking. Want to join?

# [126]

# THREE MODELS OF CHANGE

Change management or management of change. Thank God there can only be two permutations, because they are the most over-used terms in organizations. But there are three very different models of change.

Model one I call a 'Destination Model'. Here it's all about going from A to Z. Z is fixed, usually some sort of Promised Land; and A is the departure and invariably a worse place than Z. This model of change is concerned with getting to Z. The language is one of milestones, timeframes, costs and Key Performance Indicators. In other words, there's a method. I call people in this model 'The Methodists'.

I call model two a 'Journey Model'. Model two also has its destinations, but here it's more about the 'how' you get there, what you learn in the process, the experience, perhaps the engagement of people. Model two people are mostly 'travellers'. For example, people who use Appreciative Inquiry dwell here.

There is a model three. It's the 'Building Model'. This is about the building of the company's DNA. In this model, there are destinations and journeys as well, but the key focus is not just on reaching Z or on the journey to Z, but on what is being created in the new DNA. A lasting environment, an organization that has not just changed (model one) or has had a good change experience (model two), has created a new competence: change-ability. These people are builders.

The three models are very different. Traditional management uses model one. That's why we have an industry of 'change management', which in reality is more project or programme management with a proliferation of Gantt Charts. Today, however, model one, for all its merits of reaching Z (and getting yourself rewarded in the process), misses the point of sustainability. As for model two, or 'the journey'... some people in management still treat this as 'New Age Stuff' with lower credibility.

The goal of model three is to make the word 'change' redundant. In model three, 'Change Management' has become 'management'. It's a permanent ability, based on a particular behavioural DNA.

If model one is milestones and model two is experience, model three is behaviours and culture. Model one is a one-off. Model two is learning, which may or may not be a one-off. Model three is creating the long-term fabric, culture, change-ability of the organization, as opposed to just going from A to Z (but you still get to Z).

There are choices. Be clear. Forget 'change management'. Reach a destination, learn from the journey, but if you don't create long-term DNA and culture, you've lost a great deal of opportunities and possibilities.

This is the basis of Viral Change™.

# [127]

# I'LL SAY IT AGAIN: PEOPLE ARE NOT RESISTANT TO CHANGE

Am I the only one saying that?

'People are resistant to change' is the silliest statement people can make. I have written about this in many places and expressed it in many speeches. But how can I say this when we all see obvious cases of 'resistance'?

The contentious side of the statement – and this is not just a semantic trick – is the ARE. The 'are' makes resistance an inevitable trait of the human race. Look around: rapid social change, generation change, fads and fashion change, moral changes, and, above all, biological changes from birth to death. Now, try again: 'People are resistant to change'. Does it still feel right?

If anything, we ARE change. We are made of change; material, biological, psychological, spiritual. Our clay is as changeable as the weather, the seasons, the cycle of night and day. We are of a highly adaptable nature. In fact, our capacity to adapt as humans is incredible. We were born unfinished and imperfect

334

for a reason, so that we can always change and adapt. We ARE the most changeable entity under the sun.

So let's qualify: we may object to change. Sure! When? When change is imposed on us without our having a sense of relative control or space for manoeuvring. When we don't see the reason, the need. When we perceive change as a threat. When maintaining the status quo is rationally or emotionally preferred. When we feel cheated. When we are attacked and our defenses may require stillness. Keep going. Find situations.

But if we look at those situations with objectivity, we will always find not so much natural resistance per se, but reasons explaining why resistance sounds and feels preferable to change. We may or may not be right in our assessment, but that's a different question.

The trouble with most 'change management' approaches is that they start from the premise that 'people ARE resistant to change'. So when all you see is resistance, all your energy will go into overcoming that resistance. *"Here is the mountain, guys; get into climbing mode."*

'People ARE resistant to change' is simply a bad start for anything that has to do with change or leadership.

So how about this: change your default position as a leader. Start with: *"People DON'T HAVE TO RESIST this change. And if they do, let's figure out why."* Now that's a good start.

We are <u>not</u> resistant to change.

# DON'T START WITH AN ALIGNMENT OBSESSION. DISSENT IS GOOD, CREATIVE TENSION EVEN BETTER.

Let me share this scenario. It's a caricature of a common situation.

R&D wants to create a product that works. Marketing and Sales want many versions of that product, as many as possible, in order to hit as many customers as possible. Manufacturing wants to create one version, one pack, one size, one colour.

R&D does not think the way Marketing and Sales do. The 'that works' comes first, the 'that can be sold' comes later. Manufacturing does not think the way R&D or Marketing and Sales see the world. One version should be good enough for everybody. Marketing and Sales think that R&D and Manufacturing should serve their needs. After all, they understand and know what the market needs. (R&D and Manufacturing think that this is one hell of an assumption!).

Of course, I am in caricature mode, but unless you have been on a corporate sabbatical for a long time, you will recognize my points. There is a natural tension between these functions. How do we solve it? What do we need? Ah! The magic word: alignment, soon to be granted a place in the Hall of Fame of Management Commodities.

Alignment is fine, but it is usually misplaced in the 'thinking chain'. It tends to come to the party too early. Many leaders are obsessed with alignment, to the point that they expect it upfront in the decision-making process. To achieve that in the example above, it would mean that R&D needs to think like Marketing and Manufacturing and they each need to think like all the others as well. Not only that, but when this doesn't happen, you may be diagnosed with 'silo mentality' or behaving as a 'bad corporate citizen'. In the quest for good corporate citizenship, I have often seen great 'alignment' as a lowest common denominator. Everybody agrees, gets behind things, supports and aligns with what turns out to be a poor decision.

Let R&D be R&D, Marketing and Sales be Marketing and Sales and Manufacturing be Manufacturing. The creative tension is needed. Early 'alignment' in the decision-making process is a bad idea. When a client comes to me singing the alignment song and I can't find any signs of dissent, I do worry.

Change the R&D, Marketing and Manufacturing functions for any other in your company, the point is the same.

Creative tension is first, leadership decision is next and alignment comes afterwards to support and execute the leadership decision. Alignment should never be upfront.

# CORPORATE BOTOX

My local DIY/hardware store has terrible service. But now, in the tradition started by Walmart, there is an employee greeting you at the door, saying: "*Good morning, Sir. Welcome.*" The service continues to be terrible.

One of the largest consumer electronics companies in the UK has very bad in-store service. If you need product information, chances are you know more than the shop's staff. They are very good at one thing, though: reading the text on the box to you, just in case you can't read. To improve the service, they now have staff coming to you, from the corridors (sometimes even a few of them at the same time!) with a loud "*Can I help you?*" Of course, if you say yes, they will still end up reading the specifications on the box to you.

A financial services company with some history of semi-unethical behaviour has installed confidential phone lines for 'whistle-blowing' in the hope that some employees will use them and that this will prevent further embarrassments. That company has done nothing to dig up the root causes of the unethical behaviours (connected in part to the way employees are rewarded), but the 'whistle-blowing' lines have made the front-page headlines of the newspapers.

These are three different examples of Corporate Botox. The initiatives will get rid of some embarrassing wrinkles, the look will be greatly improved and everybody will 'feel' much better. But nothing really changes.

Cosmetic treatment in organizations, invasive or not, is always a possibility, I guess. And when it's part of a deeper transformation, I don't have any problem with this. On its own, it's a bit of a joke. But you'd be surprised how much airtime these 'initiatives' steal.

We must distinguish between an organizational Photoshop and the real thing. Don't be fooled by a new logo, a new uniform or a new customer language. Suspend judgment until you see if they finally stop reading the spec to you.

# REBELS!
# THEY NEED A
# CAUSE

There are always rebels and mavericks in organizations. Non-conformists, contrarian thinkers and deviants. They may be tolerated, ignored, embraced or disregarded. How an organization treats these people says a lot about its culture.

Ignoring them means that they will survive up to a point, and then they will either leave or be dismissed.

Getting irritated by them misses the point. Wasting energy 'discussing them' does not get you anywhere.

Rejecting them fully also leads to nowhere, except for maybe to their exit.

Learning from what they do is smart, particularly learning from the type called 'positive deviant'. They 'deviate from the normal way' of doing things, but achieve good results, so they can teach you a thing or two about alternative ways.

To give them a space and a role is very astute.

These are all choices...

But there are two types of rebels. One is the 'Rebel Without a Cause'. Many of you in the younger generations and those perhaps not into movies would have never heard of the 1955 film of this title, featuring the iconic James Dean. These Rebels Without a Cause seem to be rebels (or mavericks, or contrarian thinkers) just for the sake of it. They may even enjoy the visibility and airtime given to them because they are 'different'. A great deal of the contrarian pool in organizations is of this category. In some places they also fulfill another role: the trophy one. *"Look how diverse and open we are, we have people like Tim, John and Anna. That shows how different and avant-garde we are."* But Tim, John or Anna don't do much, really, other than rebel. And the organization may not be that avant-garde either.

'Rebels With a Cause' are different. They want to change or improve things, see beyond the present and apply their contrarian energy to something worthwhile. They pull people to them, engage others and are not content with the status quo. They are extremely valuable. Leaders need to make room for them.

If you have true rebels, give them a cause. The best cause is the cause of the organization, its goals, its vision, its future, not an external cause.

Give all rebels a cause. At the very least, it will be a test, for them... and for you.

# [|3|]

# INITIATIVE FATIGUE LEADING TO EXHAUSTION, LEADING TO SWITCHING OFF

Many organizations seem to run parallel initiatives at different layers, all directed at noble goals and in many cases, without talking to each other. My retrospective and un-scientific count of these in my clients of the last 10 years, showed an average of 7 per organization.

I identified Communication programmes, Employee Engagement, Values and Leadership model/programmes, Continuous Improvement, Talent Management, Change Management, Cultural Change, Innovation programmes, Idea Management, ERP implementation, Corporate Social Responsibility programmes, Diversity and Inclusion, Six-Sigma, Simplicity Programmes, Agile and several others. The situation has not changed much over the years.

344

The corporate environment today is pretty cluttered. Leaders of each initiative have a vested interest and tend to look at them in isolation. Years ago, I challenged a VP of Safety suggesting that 'our' programme should have an impact on innovation. He said, "*Maybe, but I am not in charge of Innovation*." I regularly gather similar examples in my work.

Unfortunately, it's very frequent to find that nobody, certainly not even the CEO, is able to gather all these initiatives together in a single strategy. To make sense of them all together. I often ask the question "*Where is the glue?*", but equally often I am met with simply a smile. Also, each initiative runs at its own pace, some travel very fast, some slow, some are transient, some appear and disappear for a while only to be resuscitated again at a later point in time.

The effect of this situation on the average employee is diverse. Some of it is good (it may provide additional sources of employee engagement), some of it is bad (mistaking the initiative with the overall company strategy in itself). But the most worrying effect is the saturation of channels. At some point, the mind switches off. It has enough. All becomes 'noise' and the 'signal' is indistinguishable.

Not only is this bad in its own right for all the respective initiatives, but it also injects a great, new stumbling block. From that point on, any new 'serious' initiative will have a big mountain to climb and may be mentally written off before it has even started. A cynicism creeps in. 'Here we go again' becomes the default thinking position.

I have written many times (*Disruptive Ideas*) that one of the key functions of top leadership is to de-clutter. De-cluttering is a stronger term than simplifying. It literally means killing initiatives. The slight problem is that we are asking the same leaders who clutter the environment, to de-clutter it. That said de-cluttering should be well rewarded. If keeping communication channels with employees very clean and active so that the magic currency of 'attention' can actually flow, is key to engagement, then the price to pay is to list initiatives and one by one submit them for serious scrutiny.

I call it Corporate Spring Cleaning. It works. And it has huge therapeutic benefits.

# WHEN NECESSARY, USE WORDS

Francis of Assisi is a 13th Century figure revered as a Saint by the Catholic Church. He founded three religious orders and is considered the Patron Saint of the environment and of Italy. Although always a key figure within the Catholic tradition, his name has resurfaced recently because the current Patriarch took his name: Pope Francis. As a result, there has been some renewed interest in what Francis of Assisi did and said.

The very best quote I know is this: *"Preach the Gospel at all times; when necessary use words."*

When necessary use words!

I declare Francis of Assisi the Patron Saint of Management! Or at least Behavioural Change, Viral Change™, Leadership and a few other items on the shelves of the Management Supermarket. If only we could have this motto at the entrance to the house of management, where we talk, and talk, and talk and talk...

We are 90% talk, 10% action. 90% thinking about, planning for, brainstorming about, deciding about, creating the Strategic Plan for, and a mere 10% doing.

When necessary use words!

# ONE SINGLE BEHAVIOR CAN CREATE A REVOLUTION. IT WORKS BOTH INSIDE AND OUTSIDE THE COMPANY.

This is Elizabeth Warren – American Senator, ex-Professor at Harvard, 'not running for President' (as most future runners say), the hope of American liberal democrats and the 'scourge of Wall Street' (*The Observer*, 28 December 2014):

> *"There is nobody in this country who got rich on his own. Nobody. You built a factory out there? Good for you. But I want to be clear. You moved the goods to market on roads the rest of us paid for. You hired workers the rest of us paid to educate... Now look, you built the factory and it turned into something terrific? God bless. Keep a big hunk of it. But part of the underlying social contract is you take a hunk of that and pay forward for the next kid that comes along."*

And the winner of my New Year's Behaviours Award goes to 'Pay it Forward'. That's right. Or pay back by paying forward, if you will. You get something good? Don't return something good to the sender. Give something good to others. Forward. Do once. Then repeat.

I call these single, well-defined, robust behaviours, catalytic. They have the power to create a chain reaction. You don't have to agree with Warren's political arguments to see the power of 'paying it forward'. In fact, in behavioural terms, 'paying it forward' would perhaps travel equally well across all societal and political spectra. Well, with the exception of the social-Darwinian tribes.

The concept is not new, but it has been buried in many places, achieving limited visibility. In societal terms, if multiplied and scaled up, it would be dynamite. Inside the organization it would, for example, spread collaboration at the speed of light and would shape an entire culture in weeks. Want a label? Pick one: a culture of help, people alignment, collaboration, purpose, engagement... Come on, don't be shy, carry on.

Most catalytic behaviours, such as this one, are extraordinarily simple. And because of that, they get dismissed and overlooked in the quest for complex, painful and expensive ways of creating change and culture.

My test for a 'powerful (catalytic) behaviour' is very simple and I have articulated it in my book *Viral Change*. It is the 'Imagine' test. Imagine for a second that today, a hundred or more people in your organization practiced this. Simple mathematics will tell you that, in a week you would have a revolution.

Happy New Year!

# CULTURE TRIBES, INFLUENCERS VIRAL, BROKEN WINDOWS

# OCCUPY THE CORPORATE STREETS

The traditional thinking about divisional and functional structures within organizations - which were born from the need for specialization and a clear division of labour - is that these divisions, functions or structures are well-defined. The presumption is that people will have a clear understanding of the borders between them and a clear agreement about roles and responsibilities. Cake divided: all clear.

But take a modern organization. Let's say it is a multinational business with territorial presence and multiple support functions across the board. Nowadays, other than the geography (if you are in charge of France and not, say, Italy, this is as clear as it gets) many other boundaries are far from clear.

Support functions often have far less clarity and more question marks around their identity. Corporate PR and Communication functions are challenged by Marketing. "*This is our territory*", they may say, "We *don't need you.*" These functions then challenge Marketing on brand communications. "*We are the ones who know how to communicate.*" Social media comes along and challenges everybody: *"Where do I sit, guys?"* Internal communications is challenged by modern HR and HR is in turn challenged by internal communications on Employee Engagement. *"It's mine!"*; *"No it's mine!"* R&D, Corporate and Business Development are often parallel competitors for The Product. *"We will make it"*, says R&D. *"No, we will buy it; it's cheaper than paying your salaries and we get a more decent return"*. If your corporation has a Strategic Function, the Business Units, may say to that function: *"Who do you think you are?"* Last year, when working for a multinational client, I counted seven distinct functions who all claimed to be in charge of Strategy during my interviews.

We are spending a lot of time on the 'this is mine, this is yours' game, because the borders are open and there is no point any more in appointing Border Guards: nobody will take them seriously.

Since there is no right or wrong, only capabilities, my suggestion is: Occupy the Street! Set up your tent, light the fire and display your banners. After occupying, behave like occupiers with a mission and quickly start delivering.

When I push my clients on the idea of 'occupy the space' – and, believe me, I do – I often hear, *"but surely, it is not up to us; they must tell us what space we can occupy."* 'They', the magic corporate 'they', is usually those guys on the Executive 10th floor, who have all the answers – or so the assumption goes. 'They' either don't tell you or leave you to play a strange guessing game. But the main reason why 'they' don't tell you is because 'they' don't have a clue (because nobody has, because there is no right or wrong, because these rules have not been carved in stone).

One thing 'they' (and, incidentally, you as well) don't like, is empty space. My unwritten Law of Corporate Thermodynamics says that *"Any free space will be filled, so that all the little boxes in the organization chart can take care of everything and*

**354**

*deliver comfort to leaders."* So, before the Law is applied, occupy the space, occupy the street, take charge and show the value of getting things done. 'They' may not have the energy to send in the troops to take the tents down. Who knows, 'they' may even welcome the whole thing and showcase you as an example of 'taking accountability'.

Occupy the space! If you don't, somebody will.

# [135]

# TRIBAL BRANDS THAT TEACH US A LESSON

This is an anthropology report. We've found this tribe and the people all wear the same multi-coloured clothes. They paint their faces with symbolic colours before going to the battlefield. They sing war songs. They shout. They cheer on their warriors. Animal instincts are high. The sense of identification with the tribe is enormous, practically above everything else in their lives. When successful on the battlefield, the indigenous people get inebriated en masse and often lose control. When the battle did not go well, there may be as many as thousands of natives crying, men, women and children. In extreme cases, this can turn to violence against the opposing tribe. In these circumstances, the tribal leaders are blamed even beyond the confines of the tribe. This all works through a strictly tribal, primal, animal and collective code. And the natives pay a monthly fee to belong to the tribe. This tribe also has a curious ritual: they sell their warriors to other tribes for astronomical prices. It's a football club! (Aka soccer in parts of the world with less tribal traditions of this type).

Are football club brands the prototype of brands? The Mother of All Brands? Judging by the emotions and the almost blind

356

following and belonging to a cause, surely they must rank pretty high in the Brand Cult System.

A Spanish club, not in the premier league is going through a historically bad tribal patch. They are applying modern social network analytic tools to gather massive support across the tribe and beyond, 2014- style. The full components of a social movement can be found here with the identification of influencers, their networks, their pull effect, etc. I know this, because the masters of the tribe have been in touch with me after being told by external advisers that what they were doing was pure Viral Change™ in action.

In my discussions with them, I have found a level of understanding of the rules of 'people mobilization', a deep knowledge of tools and network strategies and clarity of purpose, which I wish I could find in the average business organization. Of course they are an organization as well, but not the conventional business that I am usually called in to help. But they are genuinely and seriously looking at the business as a social movement, with mass tribal mobilization and with full mastery of social network sciences. So far they are the best business anthropologists I have come across. I am pleased our paths have crossed.

# [136]

# THE 'ABANDON HOPE' ORGANIZATION

Some organizations are little versions of Dante's Inferno, down to the sign *"Abandon hope all ye who enter here"* at the door. You may think that this is a bit dramatic, but in reality it's something you can smell. Or see the smoke from. They don't need the sign, but it is hell.

The worst hells are those that pretend not to be hells at all. Organizations with subtle toxicity in management and passive-aggressive disengagement of people, pardon my language.

Translation: management exercises power and grooms their egos; nobody else is doing much beyond their duty; people don't rush to implement decisions because they know that the lifecycle of a decision is counted in days. If one waits a bit, another decision will probably take over...

I have described this before as the Broken Windows of Management.

OK, it's kind of a benign hell, as it's not hot enough to get burnt. But it's no less hopeless. I personally prefer to be confronted with a 'hellish hell' than with a hell that doesn't look like one and sprays air freshener so that you can't small the burning. The late C.K. Prahalad had a name for these organizations: "*Calcutta in summer*".

Get the picture?

# CULTURES ARE NOT CREATED BY TRAINING.

## BARCLAYS IS MISSING THE POINT

# CULTURE

A piece in *The Guardian* on July 3rd, 2014 announced that Barclays was going to send 2,100 Compliance Staff to the Judge Business School in Cambridge to be 'trained by academics ranging from philosophers to lawyers'. Barclays was launching a multi-million pound programme that they named their 'Compliance Career Academy'. This is, of course, all happening in the context of the Banking Industry's recent history and, in particular for Barclays, the fresh allegations by the New York Attorney General, Eric Schneiderman, about fraud in their 'dark pool' trading.

Barclays chairman, Sir David Walker, confirmed that the bank already spent 300 million pounds on 'compliance'. The piece in *The Guardian* continued, by saying that the academics were going to train staff in 'truthfulness' and 'the definition of compliance'. The latter sounds like a sensible thing to do for people who are Compliance Officers. But I wonder how they got the job without 'knowing' what compliance is.

I am afraid Barclays has chosen the path of a highly sophisticated, highly prestigious, highly visible, highly educational, highly well-intentioned, highly expensive and total waste of time. A Compliance (Police) Academy will not change the culture. It's the wrong answer. Culture is behavioural. Behaviours are not taught in classrooms.

Most of the non-compliance/deviant/crossing-legal-boundaries banking problems are behavioural. They are not due to lack of rational (or even emotional) understanding. Better trained compliance police will increase the number of better educated and skilled people in compliance, with zero guarantees that this will have any effect on culture whatsoever.

Take the example of Safety. Do you think that the Deepwater Horizon oil spill in the Gulf of Mexico in 2010 (also known as the Macondo blowout), happened because BP people were not well-trained? Should we send them back to the classroom to be re-trained in Safety? Should BP double the pool of Health and

Safety officers to guarantee the avoidance of another Macondo? 'It's the culture, stupid!'

You can go back to any single 'famous disaster', including at NASA, and you will find that everybody involved was very intelligent, well-educated, well-trained and highly skilled. The last thing they would have needed was 'more training'. Every single time it comes down to 'culture'. The same applies in Banking. Increasing compliance squads in Banking, Oil and Gas, Transportation, Pharmaceuticals, etc. will never solve the culture issue.

Behaviours create culture. Behaviours are something that people exhibit and other people copy. Momentum is generated by critical mass, people within this critical mass copy each other and soon, 'a new way of doing things' becomes the norm. Behaviours belong to what I call World II, a 'pull' world (we are 'pulling' each other in behavioural terms, from the way we dress and talk, to how we push the envelope, stretch the concept of truth, speak up or not, or work within or beyond ethical boundaries). We are *Homo Imitans*. The world of communication, sensitization, awareness and education is, however, a different world. It is what I call a 'push' world or World I. This is not behavioural. It's informational. The currency here is communication. But communication is not change, certainly not sustainable behavioural change. Compliance training and legislation belong to this 'push' World I. You push messages down and hope people will behave accordingly. But the thinking behind it (*"If we just train enough people, we will be OK"*) is a fallacy.

Cultures are created in the day-to-day shaping of an environment by some subgroups of high influence, mainly on a peer-to-peer basis and in the informal organization that hosts the unwritten rules. The written rules in compliance manuals are the easy ones. These unwritten rules are the hard ones to embed into the core of the organization's fibre. You can have as much training as you want, but legislating behaviours is not a good idea. If peer-to-peer influence and behaviours take off in some wrong direction or if rewards systems don't change, the company will become a place of great compliance, safety... but with little true behavioural change.

If there is a 'push', top-down communication system that explains what needs to be done, what is acceptable and what's not (this top-down system is always necessary for this purpose; we would expect the top leadership to own this), but if, at the same time, there is no 'pull' from a bottom-up, grassroots, peer-to-peer movement to change behaviours, then the message will die. You can have as many Compliance Officers as you want, you will never shape a culture. Behaviours create cultures, not messaging and rarely threatening.

Also, compliance training, even with the Cambridge stamp, will not deal with the elephant in the room, which is "*What is the (social) purpose of banking?*" I'll tell you what it's not: to be a 'compliant industry'.

Come on Barclays! Look around (and beyond Cambridge). There has been an Arab Spring, a multitude of new social habits (from social media to smart phones), new grassroots movements everywhere, a huge increase in the volunteer sector, etc. Where was the training behind all of these? Look at the kindergartens, the playgrounds of your kids, the urban tribes... Look at how social movements are created (and culture shaping is the creation of an internal social movement), how political campaigns are run... Look at violence on the streets (on the negative side), the social spread of altruism... You'll always find these common features: no command and control, no top-down training, mainly grassroots, bottom-up, peer-to-peer influences. It's an 'infection model', not an indoctrination model. We, in business, are missing the point if we believe that 'our world' is different.

Dysfunctional banking needs an internal epidemic of integrity and ethical behaviours. This is doable, but it's not about legislating behaviours or announcing that the sky will fall in the case of non-compliance. One indicator of success? When ethics are as common in conversation as football, cricket or rugby. Unapologetically, I'll say, this is what Viral Change™ does.

Banking needs Jefferson's 'a bit of rebellion'. The problem is that no rebellion was ever born in a classroom. And revolutions need visionary leaders.

# SOLUTIONISM AS A CULTURE. PROFICIENCY IN PROBLEM SOLVING

I have become apprehensive about the use of the term 'solutions driven'. However, I am a big culprit myself. I have used it many times in my client work, particularly in my behavioural change work. I am more cautious now. In its defense, it means to have an ethos of finding a way to solve issues, to get resolution, even to be creative, imaginative, innovative, and, above all, to focus on some sort of delivery. Hard to argue against any of this. A great deal of my client engagement has taken place in a sales environment of some sort. 'Solutions driven' is always part of the furniture here and for very good reasons.

However, on the down side, when 'solutions driven' becomes a culture of <u>solutionism</u>, it means that you focus systematically on problems. If I am a solution provider, I will be looking for problems.

When your entire airtime is filled with problems, you create a culture of problems, even if your aim is to provide solutions.

There is a significant difference between a 'culture builder' and a 'solution provider'. The building mode builds, the solution mode fixes things (that are broken). For my clients, I want to have the fixing mode as a baseline, but I want to focus on building: a culture, a dream, a future, a purpose, a space in the world, a magnet for people, a brand, a portfolio of products and services. The Solution Hat is not good for the Building Aim. The hat you wear dictates what you do. A bunch of builders behave differently than a bunch of problem solvers.

If your culture is largely defined by 'solutionism', you won't build well. Many management practices, systems, fashions and approaches are based on 'solutionism': zero defects, zero tolerance, continuous improvement, variations of lean and six sigma, etc. In fact, it is hard to find an approach that does not have a dose of 'solutionism'. Many would argue that by fixing problems (of efficiency, of quality, or processes and systems) you are shaping a culture. I agree. A culture of fixing problems.

It's hard to argue against the existence of problems and the need to tackle them instead of ignoring them. If this is what you are thinking when reading this, I am not getting the point across. My contention is with the fact that it's incredibly easy for an entire culture to become infected by the focus on problem solving, and in the process of the infection, totally forgets to build. Most building can be done by providing a better, innovative way that makes the original problem irrelevant. No problem-fixing required.

When 30 people make a decision in 30 days, the problem solver looks for a more efficient way for these 30 people to work together, for a better decision-making process for 30 people, for a faster sharing of information. The builder decides to have 3 people making the same decision in 3 days. Sure, this is also a 'solution'. But all solutions are not equal. As always, there is a choice.

# FASTER HORSES

Henry Ford said, *"If I had asked people what they wanted, they would have said faster horses."*

'Faster horses strategies' are the ones that make you compete on marginal advantages (cost, speed, convenience, etc.), but don't differentiate you beyond that.

If you have horses, then being faster than your racing competitors will do a lot for you. If you have horses, but compete with cars, you are limited.

If you have cars, make sure you know them well. If your customers want a Maserati, don't try to sell them faster Fords. If they have Fords and want a faster Ford, you are OK. If you have Maserati's to sell, don't use a Ford dealership.

In the organizational development world, methodologies compete with each other. Even so-called 'change management methods' do that. They compete with each other on price, speed, number of consultants needed, number of days and rates per day. Faster horses.

People frequently ask me how Viral Change™ compares with other 'Change methodologies'. In other words, how much faster my horse is. I always have a very poor answer because Viral Change™ is not a horse. So it is very hard to say how much faster it is compared with other horses (methodologies). Viral Change™ generates large scale, bottom-up, sustainable behavioural and cultural change. In the sense that there is a process to do this, I have to say we have a method. But we don't compete on methodology. We do compete on solving complex business issues. But we don't have a faster horse, we have a completely different animal.

In the innovation world, innovation committees manage a stable of horses searching for the faster ones. People may choose to settle for the kind of 'faster horse' continuous improvement. And there may be very good reasons for this. But don't expect the value delivered by a 'faster horse strategy' to be same as the value delivered by using a Maserati.

As a leader, you have choices to make. Make sure that you know the difference between a horse, a bicycle and a Maserati.

# MY ROI IS YOUR ROI

One the biggest compliments I ever received in my consulting life, and one that I have come to appreciate more with time, was from an American CEO who told me that I was providing the 'Return on Investment (ROI)'. I remember wondering for a few long seconds what exactly he had in mind, until he explained. It was in the context of the Viral Change™ programme. Before my involvement, the company had invested in a serious, traditional, massive top-down communication and 'management of change' system, at a high cost, with a Big Consulting group. To their great concern (and little surprise to me), they hadn't seen much of a culture change happening. Viral Change™ was for them (and it is for everybody) a bottom-up, grassroots, peer-to-peer culture change at a scale... that works! And for them, it was working very well indeed.

What that CEO said made sense to the people in the room (and they were the most senior in the company). They started nodding and it seemed for a bit that they did not have anything better to say. It was kind of cold, not cool. But then I understood. They had invested. The return was negligible. My team was at last providing the ROI that they needed, admittedly by picking up the pieces of the fiasco created by others. (Incidentally, this situation is far from rare.)

369

I thought about the 'you are providing the ROI' many times afterwards and in different contexts. It became part of our internal jargon. I can think of worse ways to receive feedback from a client.

There are two questions that should be compulsory in a performance assessment review. One: *"What ROI am I providing to the company?"* And two: *"What is the ROI provided to me, the return for my (human capital) investment in this place?"* Performance appraisals should be a two-way street. Thinking and behaving like investors within the organization, makes sense. It's one of the 30 *Disruptive Ideas* in my book of the same title.

# WE ARE SO **GOOD** IN A CRISIS

Many clients have expressed this thought over the years: *"Leandro, we are so good in a crisis!"* And indeed they were!

This is the anatomy of a crisis. A crisis provides a microcosm of all possible dynamics of power and energy within the organization. People jump in and help (the true meaning of 'taking accountability'). Groups that otherwise may not talk to each other that well, rapidly join forces. Communications that may have been weak now become fluid. Individualistic people are suddenly 'all hands on deck'. Priorities are clear, objectives well-defined, time constraints evaporate... You name it, it works. I could continue with a lengthy list of other things that seem to emerge from nowhere in a crisis and make cross-collaboration, accountability and alignment (i.e. the essence of organizational life) click together almost seamlessly.

I use 'the crisis' as an experimental condition for the organization to learn about leadership, about its own real SWOTs (strengths, weaknesses, opportunities and threats) and to uncover both possibilities and people dynamics that may

371

have been hidden. It needs to be done soon after the crisis, before the organization's 'regression to normal'!

The trick is to move from 'proficiency in crisis' to excellence (or whatever you want to call it) beyond the crisis.

I have been tempted to fabricate a crisis for clients more than once, for obvious reasons...

# THE BROKEN WINDOWS OF THE ORGANIZATION

A neighbourhood with broken windows and graffiti on the walls says: *"Look how easy it is to break a window here and add neat graffiti too. It's OK, nobody cares, come on, you too can do this!"* We have all experienced degrees of this somewhere. Littering is the same. If there is rubbish on the floor, it allows you to think you can throw rubbish here too... You may choose not to, but others may.

The way this problem has traditionally been tackled in many places, is through punishment: we will find you and we will fine you. Legions of law enforcement people would be needed. And it has been tried, not surprisingly to minor effect.

At some point, a quiet Copernican revolution in behavioural terms took place. New York was one of these. Instead of deploying resources to find the perpetrators (and continue to find windows broken and graffiti on the walls and on the subways), the authorities diverted resources to fixing the windows and cleaning graffiti (notably on the New York subway). And they did this faster than the perpetrators could imagine.

In my trade, in behavioural terms, we would say they removed the reinforcement. Since any behaviour (good or bad) stays there because it is reinforced, removing the visibility of the action (the train that has been cleaned overnight, the wall that is now white, the broken window that has now been replaced – and will continue to be fixed/cleaned faster than you can break or spray-paint) defeats the purpose of the perpetrators. Removing the reward produced a resounding success!

I have applied the concept of Broken Windows to the organization for many years and first published this in an article in 2006. I have seen other people using it as well a bit more recently. In our Reboot! Accelerator, I describe it like this: *" 'Broken windows' in an organization are things (processes, routines, ways of doing things...) which are progressively 'going down-hill' without too much attention. For example, decisions may be made, but progressively not followed up on; action plans that were generated after meetings, but are no longer being read; 'requests for input' may be sent, but progressively less and less people bother to respond. They may not be 'terrible problems' by themselves, but their lack of follow-up, or implementation, or response (turning a blind eye) 'says' that it is OK to break not just a window, but more windows. Soon, the whole building could be vandalized."*

I'm sure you can create your own list. Well, imagine applying New York techniques. It should then be clear what to do.

# INTOLERANCE, DIVERSITY AND EXCLUSION: IT'S BEHAVIOURAL

'Diversity and Inclusion' (D&I) is becoming a 'policy' that many Boards have decided to adopt. This is good. However, like 'Corporate Social Responsibility' (CSR), one has to see what the terms really mean. Is it just nice language? Politically correct window dressing? Or is it real policy?

The answer lies in what you see. If D&I is mainly translated into more women on the Board, or CSR consists exclusively of a green quota of some sort, then it is window dressing. If the policies are much broader, then intentions are more serious.

Even with well-developed and broad policies, people tend to get lost in the difference between policy and behaviours. You can impose a quota for women on the Board, yet women may continue to be treated as second-class citizens elsewhere in the organization. Policy can be 'imposed', behaviours can't. Behaviours are copied in the environment. It's Homo Imitans in action. If you have a climate of intolerance, it's unlikely that a twenty-page policy document will change that.

375

Tackling 'intolerant behaviours' in the case of D&I is more important and more powerful than a D&I compliance policy. But intolerance is a defense mechanism. We can be intolerant in order to protect ourselves against a potential attack on our identity, our boundaries. When intolerance is part of the societal DNA, it is very difficult to breed any D&I in the organization.

Tolerance shaped in the schools will deal with intolerance in the community and ultimately the organization. The education system is the key.

Society knows intolerance well. Today, in Belfast, Northern Ireland, you can still see pubs with a 'Locals Only' sign, directed to keep out the large Eastern European immigrant communities. Not too many years ago, you could see the sign 'No Blacks or Irish' in English pubs. In my father's generation, immigrant Spanish workers were second-class citizens in Germany. When the Spaniards became middle class citizens in Germany, the Turks took their place. We never solved the question of intolerance, we just traded it off.

Back to the Belfast of our days, in the Catholic, nationalist Falls Road, there is a mural of Mr Gerry Adams (Sinn Fein's Republican politician historically associated with the IRA), that says 'Peacemaker, leader, visionary'. Rev. Mervyn Gibson, chaplain for the Protestant Orange Order commented: "*Sadly, it's not a memorial mural.*"

Deep-rooted intolerance will only be addressed by behaviours adopted and mimicked. On the social side, this may require fresh generations influenced by a healthy educational experience, but for organizations, surely we can be more ambitious in implementing non-negotiable behaviours instead of tolerating intolerance.

# WE WILL
## 360-FEED-BACK
# YOU

Readers of my books and clients will be aware that I am not very fond of the 360 feedback tool so frequently used in performance management in organizations.

My antibodies are not related to the principle of obtaining feedback in order to progress individually and professionally, or in order to become a better leader.

My problem with '360 feedback', where subordinates and colleagues are asked to provide anonymous input about somebody's performance and qualities, is at least twofold:

(1) In 9 out of 10 cases this tool is misused. It is used as a bad form of control, a warning for bad behaviour and even a form of punishment. You don't need to be a psychologist to understand that soliciting feedback about somebody's behaviour or traits in an anonymous but formal way is an invitation for venting, highlighting and expressing feelings that the respondent would never say to the person directly. It's often a corporate open season with a semi-Maoist finger pointing, accumulating feedback as a 'collective truth' with little room for disagreement. Very often, a 360-feedback system ignores the dynamics within the internal group and organization. Any group psychologist would be very careful when handling such feedback and they would only open discussion after they had made sure it was a safe and constructive environment. Many '360 implementations' simply end up as obtaining feedback for the sake of ticking boxes, with little thought given to what to do with the feedback itself.

(2) So, 25 people say that Jim is not very analytical (and it is implied that this is sort of bad or a weakness). What 25 people may not say, is that Jim is very 'synthetical', can put things together and provide meaning. And this may be precisely what makes Jim valuable. 25 people say Peter is inconsistent; 25 people say John is emotional; 25 people say Mary is too quick to make decisions, etc. All that, whether you like it or not, presupposes that being consistent, un-emotional and a less

quick decision-maker is desirable and good for the organization. The system presupposes an ideal normality, which is artificial. It inevitably tends to produce a comparison with a somewhat arbitrary 'ideal' type, leaving no room to decide what this 'ideal' may mean other than some dubious, general benchmarking. Jim is 3 points below the norm for managers of this kind of company based on size an industry. Really? Everybody says that Mary's communication is poor, and this is communicated to Mary with some numbers and a talk by her boss. Great!

I know I am in caricature mode here, but many years of observation (and dare I say practice) have convinced me that the misuse (abuse) of 360-feedback outweighs any of the benefits.

I've written before that my ideal angle is not 360, but 45. Now, I do believe in 45-degree feedback. 45 degrees is about the angle needed to look at oneself head on in the mirror. A mirror is the best and cheapest Leadership Development tool.

Michael O'Leary, CEO of Ryanair, notorious for his disregard for customer services of any kind, was told by his Board that the company needed to show a little bit more respect for 'the customer'. The man who once said, *"my company is the fastest at customer response; we are the fastest at saying no!"*, has now conceded that the customer is some kind of reality to be taken into account. As a result of some changes in that direction, the company has decided to invest in a Customer Relationship Management (CRM) system. O'Leary went on to say: *"We'll be getting people to register and CRM-ing the hell out of them!"*

You'll see the reason for the title of this Daily Thought. Some organizations behave in a similar way: they are '360-ing' the hell out of everybody in management. You get the picture?

In the name of anonymous and collective feedback, we are abandoning open, transparent and more difficult face-to-face conversations.

The questionnaires are easy. But it's a choice...

# SO, WHAT DO YOU DO, JOE?

Spot the differences at the dinner party or barbeque when you ask: *"So, what do you do, Joe?"*

*"I am in IT, I work for Techno"* vs. *"I am in Techno, I work in IT."*

*"I am a medical doctor, I work in PharmaTer"* vs. *"I work for PharmaTer as a medical doctor."*

*"I am a hedge fund manager, I work for InvestSmart"* vs. *"You know InvestSmart? I work there as a hedge fund manager."*

*"I am an accountant, I work for GoodsMart"* vs *"I am in GoodsMart, in finance, I am an accountant by training."*

*"I am a lawyer, I work for BankGlobal"* vs. *"I work in BankGlobal as a corporate lawyer."*

Imagine many other alternatives, for any other function. The differences are not simple anecdotal ways of expressing the same thing. The expressions are not the same. In one type, the dominance is the professional tribe (IT, medic, hedge fund, accountant, lawyer). In the other type, the company (Techno, PharmaTer, InvestSmart, GoodsMart, BankGlobal) is the dominant source of belonging. Both are compatible, for sure. But if I were the CEO of any of these companies, I'd rather have my people referring to the professional tribe after referring to the company and not before.

There is absolutely nothing wrong with the tribal-professional sense of belonging. But when projected upfront as my real persona, it means that its power, significance and identity are stronger than that of the employer's itself. Tribe: 1 – Company Brand: nil.

I have found two types of clients: those who don't get this ('don't see the difference/problem') and those who care about 'the order of things'. The latter are the ones who also care about culture. Since senior leaders, and therefore CEOs, are curators of their culture, it becomes clear very fast which ones 'see' the differences and have a preference for the company brand.

'Seeing' is the first step to interpreting and then doing something. Do you know what Joe in your company says when asked?

I wish the Employee Engagement people included this...

# TOP INFLUENCERS VS. TOP LEADERSHIP: HIERARCHICAL INFLUENCE IN THE ORGANIZATION IS HALF THAT OF PEER-TO-PEER INFLUENCE

Let me share a piece of our own research, just out of the oven.

In a 1,200-people strong pan-European company in the financial sector, we compared the power of the five person Leadership Team with the power of the top five Viral Change™ Champions (Activists) in terms of messaging, engagement and their capacity for reaching other people. We selected the Champions based on criteria for capacity to influence and establish a high connectivity within the organization. The analysis was done blind and anonymously. All staff were asked a series of seven questions to identify the colleagues who they would trust and reach out to in order to obtain some real information, or the ones who usually reach out to them for the same communication purposes.

We analyzed three steps (or 'degrees of separation') that can be considered as the closest layers of connections between individuals. One layer or step equals your immediate network, the second step reflects the connections of that immediate network and the third step relates to the connections of those connections.

The results were revealing. By step one the Leadership Team had a reach of 21 people whilst the top Viral Change™ Champions had 104. Step 2 (connections of the immediate connections) showed the Leadership Team with approximately 100 connections and the Champions with 3 times that, around 300 people. Step 3 gave the Leadership Team 250 connections as compared to 450 for the Champions. So, by step 3, the five person Leadership Team was able to reach (tap into) 27% of the workforce, whilst the five top Viral Change™ Champions reached 49%, almost half of the workforce.

The power of this data, gathered through the use of Social Network Analysis (SNA), is its inclusiveness; all people in the workforce participated and anonymity was preserved.

The results reinforce the well-established principle in Viral

384

Change™ that hierarchical power is limited when compared with the connectivity of highly influent people from all levels of the organization (Champions or Activists, in the Viral Change™ methodology). Of course, these Viral Change™ influencers need to be found, identified and eventually asked for help in shaping a cultural transformation of some sort.

Finding the real influencers inside the organization is vital to orchestrating a bottom-up, peer-to-peer transformation ('change', 'culture', new norms, etc.) It does not get better than this. Many organizations naively think that this pool of influencers matches an existing pool such as the 'Talent Management' pool. This is not the case.

In the macro-social world (for example in mass marketing), 'the death of the influencer' was proclaimed a while ago. There are reasons for that. In many social phenomena, critical masses appear without clear individual influencers. However, inside the organization, the importance of particular individuals not in the hierarchical system is clear. Internal influence of the few is alive and well.

Backstage Leadership™ is the art (performed by formal leadership) of giving the stage to those real, distributed leaders who have approximately twice as much power as the Leadership Team when it comes to influence, messaging and communications inside the firm. Similarly, these influencers shape behaviours and culture.

Our data is consistent with Edelman's Trust Barometer that ranks trust in the category 'people like me' (peers) twice as high as the trust in the CEO/hierarchical levels.

Burn those organization charts! Other than being a sort of Google map for who reports to whom, they don't say anything about the real organization. Social Network Analysis does. Then, Viral Change™ takes over to shape a culture.

# [147]

# USING NATIONAL CULTURAL DIFFERENCES TO EXPLAIN EVERYTHING IS A SMOKESCREEN FOR MANAGERIAL INCOMPETENCE

When I see that the first port of managerial justification when facing difficulties is 'cultural differences', I smell a rat. It's not that these differences do not exist, but they are the easiest things to invoke for people who don't want to think too much. If management is French, they are going to be hierarchical, the Spanish will go for long lunches and a siesta, Italians will be chaotic and passionate, Americans will be excessively matter-of-fact with zero social interest and lots of political correctness, Germans will be efficient, British will muddle through, etc. Just pick a stereotype and we're done. My glasses will dictate which reality to see. It's a very bad start. Cheap, facile and lazy!

I have seen more striking differences between one American company and another American company, than between an American company and a French company. Yes, there are some national idiosyncratic elements, but it's a bad idea to predict behaviours solely based on national stereotypes.

Experts in inter/trans-culturalism will be more sophisticated than this and will use national differences as one of many parameters.

Good management will know how to navigate through differences, national or otherwise, and will be smart enough to park stereotypes and still take into account any cultural factor. Doing business in India is not the same as doing business in Portugal. If you deal with both, you need to learn about both. But don't start with the national-cultural stereotype glasses on. See the reality first, suspend judgment, try to make sense, and then put the cultural glasses on to see if this sense increases or not.

In a multinational and global context, things are even more complex: loyalties are blurred, the sense of belonging may surprise you and the affiliate sub-culture may be different to what you expect. Incidentally, I've seen Spanish affiliates of US companies be 'more American' than HQ itself. Odd but true. This is not always the case, of course, but when this happens, you can see the desire to belong 'somewhere else' in the air people                                                                                                       breathe.

Do yourself a favour as a leader. Take a national-culture-explains-it-all sabbatical and enjoy what you see and hear. It's called Leading Beyond The Passport.

# CORPORATE CULTURE AS A SOCIAL MOVEMENT

Large scale mobilization and alignment of people, united through common goals, but yet everybody is in different and diverse roles with a large proportion of volunteers: I am describing a typical social movement. But I want to describe corporate culture in the same way.

We need to think of corporate culture as a social movement. There is a lot to be gained by this. Don't think of corporate culture as a large classroom where everybody gets messages and is trained. Or as the sum of all regulations and policies. Or as a set of labels that somebody has created: entrepreneurial, mature, authoritarian, engineering, agile, customer-focused, etc.

Culture needs a shared understanding, a common language, a common sense of purpose and a shared commitment to action. It does not need a people-cloning system, but rather an environment where people can share their dreams; where company dreams are compatible with personal dreams. They don't have to be the same.

Business organizations that have developed their thinking based on the teachings of traditional business schools are at a disadvantage. The best source of inspiration and learning on corporate cultures comes from studying social movements. Many well-orchestrated political campaigns have a lot to teach us.

The Obama campaigns of 2008 and 2012 have been fundamental to understanding large-scale mobilization. I have dissected them in detail through the lens of my organizational work. It has convinced me of two things: (a) Viral Change™ (behavioural, bottom-up, grassroots, peer-to-peer orchestration of large-scale change) is the modern answer to organizational and cultural change; (b) 90% of my (large) traditional organizational development library is as relevant as the telegraph is in today's communications.

# [149]

# THE HALL OF FAME OF MISTAKES

In a recent cultural assessment that we conducted, we analyzed the treatment of mistakes within the corporation. This is a great diagnostic tool that tells you a lot about the DNA of the organization. It's one of the 12 diagnostic pieces we use in our Reboot! Accelerator programme.

One typical answer, paraphrased millions of times, is: *"Mistakes are OK as long as they stay within the team"*. The problem with many mistakes in the organization is that they are often too secret. Kept behind closed doors for fear that they could backfire on us. We have to be sympathetic to this approach, since too many people have been penalized for their mistakes.

The nastiest cases are the ones where leaders have said that mistakes were OK when obviously they were not, and people have ended up blamed and punished. Even worse is the realization that people at the top of your organization have never made a mistake, simply because they have also never taken a serious risk.

If you are really serious about learning from mistakes, you, as leader, need to do two things: One, make them public. Two: make yours public. Preferably in reverse order.

'The Hall of Fame of Mistakes' is incredibly cathartic. Publicize: "*My Screw-ups of the month are...*" and you will de facto declare that it is OK to make mistakes and that you can now draw as many learnings as you can from them.

Do this if you are a CEO, senior leader or in top management and invite others to do the same. You won't believe the amount of fresh air that will come through those windows that you have just opened.

# [150]

# TRUST IS LIKE PREGNANCY. YOU CAN'T JUST HAVE A LITTLE BIT OF IT!

Statements such as 'I don't trust him too much' in reality, mean I don't trust him at all. The 'too much' is a softener that we include to make the statement a little bit questionable, to give the vague impression there is still some hope of full trust.

But trust is a funny non-linear thing, excuse my language. It takes time to build, sometimes at a considerable effort. It reaches maturity, stabilizes, but can then suddenly go out the window following even just a small breach. Non-linear. Most non-linear effects are associated with the expression 'it's not fair!' For example, it is not fair that you delivered A, B and C in a superb way and you only failed to deliver D, but still your trust drops at the speed of light. Life is not fair (life is not linear).

Trust is built in different ways, but, at the core, it's always a game of vulnerability. Can I make myself vulnerable to Peter and know that Peter will not abuse this? Can I be wrong and not be told off or penalized? Can I make mistakes and not be sacked? Can I disclose what I don't know, how full of doubt I may be, my question marks, my homework not done, my declaration of un-preparedness, and still be confident that Peter, or John or Mary will not jump on me, disclose my weakness to others or put me in their black books or simply lose faith in me?

When thinking about trust, I am very binary: Yes or No. I know that anything in between is more an expression of hope (in either direction) than a reality.

# DISRUPTIVE:
## A WORD FOR ALL SEASONS IN NEED OF A HOLIDAY

Jill Lepore, author, staff writer at *The New Yorker* and Harvard professor of American History, has created a little storm, which thanks to her New Yorker pulpit, did not stay contained within the academic class. She has dared to challenge every single bit of her fellow Harvard colleague, Clayton Christensen's theory of Disruptive Innovation in her article *The Disruption Machine. What the gospel of innovation gets wrong._*(The New Yorker, 26 March 2014).

Here is one of her gems:

*"Disruptive innovation is a theory about why businesses fail. It's not more than that. It doesn't explain change. It's not a law of nature. It's an artifact of history, an idea, forged in time; it's the manufacture of a moment of upsetting and edgy uncertainty. Transfixed by change, it's blind to continuity. It makes a very poor prophet."*

Mr Christensen is not amused and calls Lepore's piece *"A criminal act of dishonesty — at Harvard, of all places."* Note: the 'of all places' reminds us, the mere mortals, that we inhabit 'the other places'.

Lepore is bright and razor sharp. Christensen can't believe that his empire of 'Disruptive Innovation' (and it is an academic, consulting, publishing, cult empire) can be challenged. Almost nobody has done it so far.

Regardless of the academic and historical scrutiny, and suspecting that the conversation will go back and forth for a bit (as we are used to seeing in 'the other places'), one thing is at the core of the issue: the absurd overuse and ubiquitous utilization of the word 'disruptive', making it overworked, trying and even exhausting. It has been used to explain everything. If you used to go to the cafeteria for lunch and now you get a sandwich from a newly installed vending machine, chances are somebody will call this 'disruptive' (the vendors, the decision, the policy), even if the only real disruption is in your stomach and your taste. 'Disruptive' has taken over a great deal of airtime in the managerial sphere. It's now a word for all seasons.

The reality is that you will find a spectrum of uses: The ones who say Skype is a disruptive technology (accurate), the ones who use disruptive to describe many forms of change (which may or may not be seriously disruptive) and the trivial changes such as the vending machine type described above. Kevin Rose of *The New York Times* begs us to put a stop to this in his article: *Let's All Stop Saying 'Disrupt' Right This Instant.* (June 2014) As you can see, some people are desperate. Jim Naughton of *The Observer/The Guardian* also seems distressed: "*Clayton M. Christensen's theory of 'disruption' has been debunked. Can we all move on now, please?*" (July 2014) (Although there is no single line is his article where he explains why 'it has been debunked'.)

I am personally leaning towards Mark Twain here and think that the death of Disruptive Innovation has been largely exaggerated. What we are desperate for is the end of its use as a cliché that 'explains everything'.

In 2008, I myself wrote a book entitled *Disruptive Ideas* but, thank God I gave a definition in the first pages!

*"Disruptive [management] ideas are those that have the capacity to create significant impact on the organization by challenging standard management practices. They share the following characteristics:*
*They are simple.*
*There is a total disproportion between their simplicity and their potential to impact on and transform the life of organizations.*
*They can be implemented now.*
*You can implement them at little or no cost.*
*They are most likely to be contrarian.*
*They are also most likely to be counterintuitive.*
*They pose a high risk of being trivialized or dismissed.*

**396**

*They can spread virally within the organization very easily.*

*You only need a few disruptive ideas to create big transformation without the need for a Big Change Management Programme. The impact of a combination of a few is just like dynamite."*

And we run an Accelerator programme based on those 30 ideas of the book. No apologies! I gave my definition upfront.

It's clear that Language Takeover is a feature of management thinking. The warnings about 'Disruption' are timely and sound. That's far from writing the death certificate for the concept. But please, Mr Christensen and Ms. Lepore, do continue the back-and-forth for a bit longer. There are aliens outside of Planet Harvard who appreciate the show.

# [52]

# IN NEED OF NETFLIX' IRRATIONAL LOGIC

The American version of the British *House of Cards* (book, then TV series), is a fine piece of art. Kevin Spacey is the perfect Washingtonian Machiavelli and his wife the perfect Washingtonian Lady Macbeth. Series 1 had 13 episodes and Series 2 another 13, each of them close to one hour long.

The series will be remembered for its quality and string of nominations and awards. But also for the disruptive thinking of their producers and buyers. The series was bought by Netflix, the on-demand streaming media company. Unlike other TV series there was no pilot. In fact, instead of releasing one episode a week, as would happen with conventional TV channels, Netflix released all 13 episodes in one go, resulting in a 13-hour long film. And they did this twice, with a third series now waiting in the wings!

Many people called Netflix producers crazy. The TV companies certainly thought Netflix was completely mad, even 'irresponsible'. Netflix subscribers have since reached 33 million and counting, in the US alone. It's not only a big success: they have also created a precedent. Many others will

398

follow. The entire economic model for TV sitcom has been shaken up. For a small monthly subscription of just under 10 US dollars a month, not only can one watch a myriad of movies and TV series, but in the case of the House of Cards, an entire season in one day. With some coffee.

We could do with some 'Netflix thinking' in organizations. For each 'established' way of doing things and for each unchallenged practice, we need to ask ourselves, is there a different way? Better? Disruptive? What if? It almost doesn't matter if you have a good answer or not. The simple discipline of 'thinking Netflix' would bring fresh air into organizational life.

And the training for this disruptive thinking is cheap: practice the thinking!

IN FRIENDS, BUDDIES, PALS, MATES, I TRUST.
TRUST IN ORGANIZATIONS IS HORIZONTAL
OUR MANAGEMENT SYSTEMS ARE VERTICAL
"HOUSTON, WE HAVE A PROBLEM!"

Get yourself a copy of the Edelman Trust Barometer. The Edelman company produces an excellent annual report on trust (organizations, industries, geographies...) and year after year, with some minor variations, the lowest source of internal organizational trust (for the purposes of 'believing' what's going on with your company) is the CEO. Let's be kind. It means the top hierarchy, not only that absolutely charming and well-mannered CEO who is on TV from time to time. And of course, not <u>your</u> CEO.

The highest source of trust, however (with a glitch in favour of 'academics' last year), is 'people like me'. That's it, people like you and me, one of us, our horizontal tribe, the ones we talk to everyday and talk football or cricket or baseball with, the ones who take their children to similar schools, more or less same age, 'my mates'. You may be one rank above (or below) me or two, but that does not really matter around the water cooler, or in the cafeteria, or car park. My peers.

Here's the trick. If my Super Vice-President comes to me and tells me that we have to go South, I will say OK. Perhaps I will ask why, but I know I will end up going South. The CEO thinks South is good. The Strategic Plan says that South is good. However, I am not sure about the South. Actually, I think South is a lousy option. Why South for goodness sake?

If you, my peer (mate, water cooler friend, car park talker, school run sharer, co-smoker, tribal member, colleague in the same division, free psychotherapist and somebody 'I know well'), come to me and in the middle of a football game, or school run, or holiday, or dreadful journey say to me, *"By the way, we really must go South"*, then my brain may suddenly be aroused by the unexpected. I may have one or two questions such as *"Are you on something?"*, but the chances of me now considering that, at the very least, South is a very reasonable, maybe even extraordinary destination, are very, very high indeed. In fact, a few hundred points above the same message coming from my Super Vice-President. I expected him to support South, but I did not expect you to share your belief in South with the same sincerity as in our twenty other conversations. Call it trust (Edelman does) or legitimization, or (for me) comfort, but all of a sudden, the South is very credible.

If on top of 'we really must go South', you say to me that you are actually going South yourself, the chances of my doing the same are even higher. And most of this process may even be unconscious.

Nothing in our traditional view of the organization, let alone the supreme representation of the corporations' plumbing system, the organization chart, says anything about the peer-to-peer (horizontal) mechanisms. In fact, they are ignored. The emphasis is vertical. You to your direct reports, your direct reports to their direct reports and so on. Ditto in the public sector or societal campaigns: doctors to patients, social workers to dysfunctional families, priests to immigrants and community leaders to gang members.

In Viral Change™, activists work through informal networks of recovered patient to patient, ex-dysfunctional family to dysfunctional family, settled person to immigrant and ex-gang member to violent street gang members.

The power of peer-to-peer networks is formally called to arms in Viral Change™ programmes. One heading in my book *Homo Imitans* reads 'youth to youth, grannies to grannies' to make the point of this transversal power.

(Good CEOs and top leaders react: "*Fantastic! Now we know who has the power!*")

# THE PHARMA COMPANY THAT FORGOT TO DISPLAY ITS **PURPOSE**

A few months ago, I was in the lobby of a global pharma company waiting for my appointment. I sat in front of several big flashing screens of the type one can now see in the reception area of many companies. I was curious to see what was displayed. The content was constantly moving, pretty fast, with pictures of smiling people and other things like buildings that looked like scientific labs and manufacturing plants.

The gentle bombardment was constant and very rich in data. There you had the names of the medicines they sold, their market share, the number of countries in which they operated, the number of people dedicated to R&D, the different nationalities of people in the workforce, the award for employee engagement and a few lines of what seemed to be their mission statement.

My curiosity grew when I felt something was missing. Since I was watching from some distance, I thought it might be that I was not looking properly. I got closer to the panels, but the panorama only changed a bit. Now I could see a Stock Market ticker showing the stock price of the company, proudly exhibiting an arrow point upwards and a plus sign followed by the number 0.5.

There was no mention of number of people treated (which is not the same as number of medicine units sold) or how the medicines were affecting people's lives. One of the medicines in their portfolio is actually life-saving. For a life-saving drug, you would have thought that it would be absolutely natural to say how many lives have been saved. Nope.

I felt embarrassed. Unfortunately, this is not uncommon. We see far more displays of operational performance than of purpose, whether on LCD screens or in a less digitalized medium. By 'purpose' I don't even mean 'high purpose'. There may be other not so dramatic purposes in many industries, but there is always one. But for a pharma company to forget the number of lives they have saved is pretty bad.

The very few times I have discussed this kind of thing with other people, I find myself in a strange minority. I am told, "What? *You don't like saying that people are making money? Or do you have a problem with profits? What's wrong with making money?*" Which are kind of strange reactions because the last time I checked I saw that I was not going around dressing like, or posing as, Saint Francis of Assisi.

The purpose of a company is to make money, people say. More people than you think. Is that it? The following human activities make money: a grocery, arms trade, a casino, an insurance company, a supermarket, illegal human traffic, the mafia, a bank. Should I carry on? This commonality does not make them all equal.

It seems that we are still apologetic about, or embarrassed by the word 'purpose'. Perhaps we have grown so sceptical of 'mission and vision statements' that anything that smells slightly 'soft' (as some people still say) is simply suspicious.

What a shame that we sometimes cannot articulate, clearly and loudly, the purpose of the organization and its space in the social world.

The example that I shared came from a real pharma company, but you can extrapolate the argument to any other company and sector. High purpose, purpose, small purpose? Please tell us – clearly, without whispering – why you exist.

# EPILOGUE

# IN PRAISE OF
# BORDERS

## THE BORDER DIET: A FITNESS PLAN FOR THE SELF AND THE SOUL.

*My 'Director's Cut' of a TED talk given at TEDx East London under the theme of 'Society Beyond Borders' on Saturday 18th of January 2014*

If you go to a little town in Ireland called Pettigo, you will find that it is split in two, right in the middle. Half belongs to 'The South', the Republic of Ireland and half to 'The North', Northern Ireland, part of the United Kingdom. Many countries in the world know about borders and boundaries, and history has been written on the back of them, but I think Ireland would rank very high on the scale for a true anthropology of the border. They know about borders. Borders which used to have walls and towers and guns.

Today, the border in Pettigo is only marked by a different colour of the road. One line, two shades of grey on the ground. That's it. The border is gone. Perhaps a reminder of hope for the many other borders with walls and guns that still remain in many places in the world; still writing history, very often a history of suffering, separation and shattered dreams.

When I was growing up in Spain, traveling abroad was not a given like it is today. I did not go abroad or use a passport until I started Medical School. I was 18. Then, I did cross the border with friends. It was an exhilarating experience. We went to Andorra, the tiny country next door! Actually you could see a sign saying 'Welcome to Andorra!' We were really abroad! We could not believe it!

Things have changed quite a bit since. Last year, in 2013, I took 45 airplanes. Believe me, a complete anti-climax compared with my first trip to Andorra, which was then followed by the far more adventurous France. We just kept going north following the main road, crossing the next border! That was a crossing of liberation and identity, a small rite of passage still stuck in my memory. For us, young adults of the Spain of the seventies, France did not mean romantic weekends in Paris; it was a place for watching films we could not watch in Spain and buying books which we could not buy on our side of the border. The border was a big deal.

# EPILOGUE

Today, we have all come to celebrate the freedom to move around, not to be constrained either by observation towers and machine guns, or by other boundaries of race, gender or ideology. This has become a noble aim of rights and freedom. Any idea we can attach the words 'without borders' to has a head start. From 'Doctors without borders' to 'Basketball without borders' and anything in between, we have praised the borderless world so much, for very good reason, that we have unconsciously made any border bad. I am here to reclaim some borders.

Something has happened in the last generations. The greatest border revolution was not achieved through any Geneva treaty or a peace process. There was no war or people in streets and plazas. The world became digital. And this digital world has turned almost everything upside down. The changes in our world are almost Copernican. The new human landscape is almost unrecognizable, although the current generations of digital natives don't see it like this. We, the analogues know the difference!

The revolution has brought both immense progress and interesting paradoxes. Because the side of progress is so overwhelming, the paradoxes don't tend to get much quality airtime. Here are a few:

Distance is gone. The distance between my next-door neighbour and a friend in New Zealand is the same. Distance is not measured in miles or kilometres. If anything, it may be measured by the bandwidth of your internet. But despite the death of distance, we have not necessarily gained in proximity to each other. Nobody has put it better than Sherry Turkle of MIT in the title of her latest book *Alone Together*. The illusion of proximity is amplified by the epidemic of Full Disclosure of Myself driven by ubiquitous social media and the fall of the Privacy Wall. Somebody said that the young generations don't care about Big Brother, what they are really afraid of is Big Mother, when she asks you to be her friend on Facebook! That

<u>is</u> a border! Closeness is now a numerical concept (with some digitalized faces talking or texting), an idiom without Royal or Language Academy.

We have become hyper-connected but not hyper-collaborative. Connectivity is not collaboration, but we tend to dangerously use them interchangeably, as if they were close in meaning. Hyper-connectivity allows us to participate in the social plaza by the not too onerous movement of a finger-click that allows us to like and follow – creating a new generation of armchair activists. To the critics of this clicktivism, others respond that this is good because at least it facilitates awareness and sensitization to issues. Which is true, if what you want is to create legions of hyper-sensitized and hyper-aware voyeurs.

Technology also makes us rich in time and space, yet we suffer from the greatest time famine. The anytime-anywhere landscape came with a roadmap to the Promised Land of the milk of free time and the honey of work-life balance. As other travellers of the biblical desert discovered a long time ago, there is no milk or honey at the destination. Moses would have been fired today.

The digital revolution has also installed the word 'instant' in the presidential palace. Today, this word defines almost all expectations for anything in life. So children grow up with less and less sense of deferred gratification, which is what forms character. If you could get instant coffee in analogue times, you can get instant knowledge now in the digital one. Today, answering a question in your children's homework may be as intellectually complex as cutting and pasting. 'I know how to' has replaced 'I know why'. Knowing where the answer is may give your child an A, even if the child does not know what the answer is. Critical thinking is outsourced to the algorithms of Google. Re-search is a Google search you have done twice. We are the mini-Gods who can reach Ithaca on screen.

# EPILOGUE

Of the winners and losers, we tend to see the winners because they are so pervasive and 'obvious'. But the roots of the word obvious mean 'in the way'. The shining progress gets in the way of a critical and healthy look at the deep impact on the way we think, the way we do things, the way we are, ourselves, our Self.

The great Spanish philosopher Ortega y Gasset is often known because of a single sentence in one of his books: "*I am I and my circumstances.*" That was the thirties. Today, Ortega would say, "*I am I and my Facebook tribe, my followers, or fans, or my likes. Or perhaps I am I and my avatars.*" Ortega moved the border of the self adventurously for his time, although his existentialist statement may seem banal today. Today, the borders of the self have moved again, this time far away, perhaps to terra incognita.

When I was a practicing psychiatrist, 'multiple personality disorder' was something unhealthy in the manual. The digital world has blurred the borders of identity. Identity here <u>is</u> multiple (you can be anybody and many bodies in Digital United), yet you are not mentally ill. Having multiple personalities is now healthy. Adolescents in particular today form several simultaneous digital identities. Psychological borders have been blurred. I challenge anyone to find this in a standard Psychology manual.

Once upon a time, in the analogue era, writing a Declaration of Independence was perhaps the climax of identity and purpose. It was a Declaration of Borders. Today, independence is dead. Nothing that we do as individuals, or employees in an organization, or as a group, or as a country is independent. Like the multiple domino effects that we see in the markets, insulation and independence are only as real as dreams. The Ortegan conspiracy is alive.

These days I ask my business clients to write down their Declaration of **Inter**dependence, either of themselves or the organizations they lead. Once clarified that I did not make a spelling mistake, very often the scales fall from their eyes and focus switches from preserving independence to mastering the interdependence.

In the individual sphere, we declare our triumphant freedom and independence – remember, mini-Gods are really, really free – yet we surrender our privacy to thousands of 'friends' we have hardly met, becoming dependant on an audience. Aside from the lack of privacy, this networked world that we belong to, makes us more inter-dependent, particularly in one way: more tribal. Belonging to a tribe (urban, digital, cause...) is often stronger than to a country or even to being a 'global citizen'.

My tribal brother or sister is primarily 'somebody like me'. So I rely more on what other 'patients-like-me' say of my illness than on what doctors say. Tribal websites and portals ('patients like me', being one of them) are growing. Trust is horizontal.

In my work as an organizational architect, we see a similar phenomenon. People trust more what 'people-like-me' say about the organization than what the CEO tells them. This is reflected year after year in the Edelman trust barometer: around 30-40 % trust in the CEO; around 60-70% in the 'people like me 'category (read: one of us, my mates, my colleagues, comrades, my horizontal, transversal tribe...).

The old analogue world was very good at creating top-down authority. The digital world is horizontal. The analogue citizen looked up and down, the digital citizen looks sideways. The power is now in the tribe. Peer-to-peer trust is greater than hierarchical trust. What the social network says and likes is my reality. The world has become flat. The truth is a web of beliefs. All my Facebook monkeys can't be wrong.

From all 'border issues' that have been blurred, or opened, or taken down in the digital, networked, horizontal, sideways, tribal, instant, time-less, space-less world, one above all worries me: the one of the self and the soul. I suggest that the Self Without Borders is the 21st Century's tragic illness. Not everybody will catch it in full, but symptoms are worryingly widespread already.

It seems that more and more people are now living in what the late Irish poet, John O'Donohue, called 'inner eviction and outer exile'. The self is forced to come out and reach the audience, the nomadic tribe, the Promised Land of the likes and followers where the milk of belonging and the honey of acceptance is waiting for you. It's not just a little stroll around the house, it's a full outing and potential moving out. Taken to the extreme, it's permanent exile. This means you could end up in the Intensive Care Unit for the Self and the Soul.

The big problem with Self-exhibitionism and self-eviction is that it depletes your inner goods. To be human is to give something of yourself. When there is no stock left and all is sent to the market, to the Grand Bazaar, there is nothing left to give. I know people who tell me 'I am an open book', 'I have no secrets', 'I am transparent', most often said with pride. They worry me. They have exhausted their stocks of identity. Their borders are gone. The cult of openness, transparency and self-eviction to the outer-exile unsettles me. I often wish for them that they preserved a bit of opacity.

So, I had to say something! Using my medical background – just kidding – I have created the climax of all recipes: a diet. It's called The Border Diet: A Fitness Plan for the Self and the Soul. I am still working on the branding! The diet has the following points:

1. Have a list of secrets, make an inventory, keep them. Review them monthly. Having no secrets is a symptom of Self-depletion. There are sacred secrets of your soul and in your soul. They are your real friends, because they are the closest to you. The problem is that in the

Full Disclosure pseudo-nirvana regime, the word secret has become associated with bad. It should not be.

2.  Take social media sabbaticals. Make yourself not just 'unavailable' (this is the analogue term), but 'un-discoverable' (digital). Bluetooth devices ask you to switch them (or not) to 'discoverable' mode so that other devices can recognize and 'pair' with them (my apologies to digital natives, I know you know that, but I am writing here for analogues as well). So learn to make yourself 'un-discoverable' from time to time. Or be selective to whom you make your Self discoverable to. And how much, and for how long.

3.  Drop Pilates, take Pascal classes. Pascal said that "*all of humanity's problems stem from man's inability to sit quietly in a room alone.*" That has not changed since the 17th Century. If anything, it is incredibly more difficult today. The 21st Century human can't 'sit': we are restless, attention deficit disorder animals. 'Quietly' is hard in a 24/7 loud world. The 'room to sit alone' is crowded with nomadic audiences and populations of different sorts. But, it's all about practising!

4.  Make an inventory of assets you can give to others: start with time, ideas, attention, care. Keep stocks high. Make sure you don't give too much at a time. Perhaps in small quantities only to people you know and those who need you. Then increase the dose progressively. Many relationships fail because they result in mutual depletion instead of mutual enhancement.

5.  Practice daily silence. Start simple: radio off, earphones off. Despite common belief, it is possible. Simultaneous multi-channel, multi-stimulation of the senses is not needed for survival. Silence will help you listen to your Self, and who knows, even beyond. It's not for nothing that silence has been called God's language.

6. Practice stillness. Stop moving, jogging, going to the gym. Well, not all the time. Don't do anything, I repeat, anything, for a good 30 min a day. Try. It won't kill you. Notice I have not said meditation. Meditation is doing something.

7. You would not choose to be in a room full of smoke or in a contaminated nuclear area. Mental pollution is much worse than either of these. It's the greatest digital health hazard. Avoid systematic mental exposure to trivia in the same way you would avoid breathing smoke.

8. Don't be open, transparent and exhibitionist. You are fooled by your ego. Hard to accept as it is for many people, nobody really cares about you checking in to the airport of X, having cereals Y for breakfast today or just changing your cover photo in Z. You are mainly reporting to yourself what your Self knows already. You've probably reacted cynically more than once when put on hold by a voice telling you that 'your call is important to us', but obviously not as important as actually taking your call. Imagine the world saying, "*keep posting, your posts are important to us.*" Get the picture?

9. Reconcile with your borders, protect your distances and go back to your inner house. Then you can give from within. But you need to protect your Self from the borderless world of all windows open, all doors open. The Self may catch a cold.

10. Then, go back to number one.

As with any diet, it does not come free of hassle and effort. It needs practising, commitment, resolution and those other things you apply to your physical health.

Reclaim your borders. You may even feel bad, or selfish or guilty. This is normal. Drop the guilt. Give yourself a break, a good recurrent border break.

Because this is seriously about your Self.

You are you and your borders.

# ABOUT THE AUTHOR

Leandro Herrero, a psychiatrist by background, spent many years in hands-on leadership positions in global companies before founding The Chalfont Project Ltd, a leading consulting group of organizational architects. He has pioneered Viral Change™, an unconventional and very successful way of creating large-scale behavioural and cultural change. He leads the Viral Change™ Global network of companies.

As a speaker, Leandro Herrero has won the highest recognition from many audiences, big and small, at public forums and in-house events. That includes the Gran Davos Award in a World Communication Forum. He has also presented at TEDx in London with great reception.

As an author, he has published several books on management of change and leadership. These include *Viral Change*, *Homo Imitans*, *Disruptive Ideas*, *New Leaders Wanted* and *The Leader with Seven Faces*.

As a consultant, he works with organizations of many sizes at different levels: from Board and top management and leadership teams to staff in Business Units. His consulting work focuses on management of change, leadership, human collaboration, organizational branding and innovation. He has designed a suite of 'Accelerators' to speed up change, innovation and people alignment in organizations.

# ”DAILY
## THOUGHTS
### BY LEANDRO HERRERO
24/7, 08:00 a.m GMT @leandroherrero.com

Leandro Herrero writes a daily blog 'Daily Thoughts' at **www.leandroherrero.com**.

To be part of this community of However Thinkers and to make sure you don't miss your daily dose:

Subscribe through the site to receive it via email,

Follow us on Twitter: @LeandroEHerrero, @chalfontproject, @LHDailyThoughts

or via LinkedIn Pulse

# HOWEVER

LEANDRO
HERRERO
WORK COULD BE REMARKABLE

Explore possibilities beyond the book at
**www.howeverbook.com**.

Through this site, you can order copies of the book. You can also organize webinars, short or long consulting sessions, keynotes and workshops around the book or other topics related to people and organization. And so much more. These engagements are led by the team at The Chalfont Project. The book is also available in all major online stores.

# THE CHALFONT PROJECT

## ORGANIZATION ARCHITECTS

BUILDING REMARKABLE ORGANIZATIONS

## WE ARE YOUR ORGANIZATIONAL ARCHITECTS

If you want to build a remarkable organization or challenge your status quo, we are your organizational architects. If you need the best leadership, if you want a collaborative environment, if you want to master change or instil radical management innovation: we promise you will have them. Work with us. We won't tell you things just because you want to hear them.

We will advise you, work with you and we will make a difference. We don't do 'small difference' – if this is what you have in mind, don't hire us. We work with people with ambition, who see possibilities, who have a sense of urgency and who want to make a difference in their worlds – teams, leaders, companies, society. Also, we don't do misery. Pain is sometimes inevitable, but misery is always a choice. (Not ours though, life is short.)

*Warning*: we have a bias for behaviours in everything we do. Others may ignore them in favour of processes or structures, but for us there is no change of any kind unless there is behavioural change. So, talk to us.

**www.thechalfontproject.com**

**+44 (0) 1494 730999**

*Leandro Herrero is the CEO of The Chalfont Project Ltd*

422